JAMESTOWN EDUCATION

inClass Reader

TREK 3

Jamestown
READING
NAVIGATOR

Mc Graw Hill **Glencoe**

New York, New York   Columbus, Ohio   Chicago, Illinois   Peoria, Illinois   Woodland Hills, California

JAMESTOWN EDUCATION

 Glencoe

The McGraw-Hill Companies

Copyright © 2007 by The McGraw-Hill Companies, Inc. All rights reserved. Except as permitted under the United States Copyright Act, no part of this publication may be reproduced or distributed in any form or by any means, or stored in a database or retrieval system, without prior written permission of the publisher.

Send all inquiries to:
Glencoe/McGraw-Hill
8787 Orion Place
Columbus, OH 43240-4027

ISBN-13: 978-0-07-861038-7
ISBN-10: 0-07-861038-9

Printed in the United States of America.

2 3 4 5 6 7 8 9 10 110 11 10 09 08 07 06

Contents

Unit 2   How Can Music
       Make a Difference?..................37

Unit 7   How Do I Measure Success?.......193

How Do Sports Affect Lives?

Sports hold a mirror to our lives. They are more than entertainment; they are the struggle of winning and losing. Playing sports requires a concentrated mixture of skill, teamwork, confidence, and self-reliance.

Sports not only reflect life, they can also affect life. Sports teach life lessons. By participating in sports — getting involved as a player or as a watcher — we learn to value rules and fair play. Sports teach us how to succeed and how to pick ourselves up when we fail.

From AD/HD to Everest:
The Story of Danielle Fisher

Danielle Fisher took up mountain climbing to help her ability to focus on one thing. As her attention improved, so did her climbing skills. With fresh goals and renewed confidence, she conquered the highest mountain peaks in the world.

More Information
Mount Everest is the highest mountain in the world at 29,035 feet above sea level. It is in the Himalayas between Tibet and Nepal.

On June 2, 2005, twenty-year-old Danielle Fisher became the youngest American ever to reach the **summit** of the world's tallest peak: Mount Everest. On its own, this is an amazing **accomplishment.** For Danielle Fisher, though, it's just one of many.

---

summit the highest point, such as the top of a mountain
accomplishment the act of achieving a special goal

8

As a young girl, Danielle Fisher loved to run free outside her family's home in Bow, Washington. She whiled away hours exploring the land. Danielle didn't need toys; she was happy to be out in the fresh air. "The gully and stream have been my playground my whole life," she remembers.

Danielle felt free outside, but in school she felt trapped. "I was never really great at school. I was smart, but easily distracted and had a hard time turning in assignments." Eventually, Danielle turned to her teachers and parents for help.

Finally, in sixth grade, Danielle was diagnosed with AD/HD — Attention Deficit/Hyperactivity Disorder. She began taking medication to help her focus. The medicine improved her concentration, and she received support from friends, family, and a **counselor.**

What Do You Know?
What do you know about AD/HD? Do you know anyone who has it?

counselor a person who gives advice or help

9

Danielle knew she couldn't rely on other people forever, though. "You have to find a balance between knowing that you need help and making an effort to push through yourself." She realized that medicine, family, and friends could all help her but that she would also need to work hard to do the things she wanted to do. "I realize that medication helps me. It certainly makes it easier to focus, but I also have to make the personal effort to make my dreams possible."

Danielle believes that it is important for people with AD/HD to set goals for themselves — not just any goals, but goals that will **motivate** them to stay focused. She says, "Discover what your **passions** are, because when you are enjoying what you are doing, or working toward something you are excited about, you will be able to focus on that goal."

Fortunately, Danielle found the goal that excited her. The summer before her sophomore year of high school, Danielle overheard her dad, a lifelong **mountaineer,** talking about climbing Mount Baker. She decided to give it a try, and that summer she completed her first climb.

---

motivate to provide a reason or cause for someone to do something
passions strong likings for certain activities
mountaineer a person who climbs mountains

At first, Danielle did not enjoy climbing. "I hated it! It was like work," she recalls. It was physically and **mentally** demanding, but she **persevered.** Danielle continued to go on trips with her dad that summer. She climbed mountains such as Mount Adams and Mount Rainier. After summiting Mount Rainier, she was hooked.

Following a father-daughter climb of Aconcagua, the highest mountain in the South American Andes, Danielle set her **ultimate** goal: She would attempt to summit each of the world's six other highest mountain peaks.

English Coach
Many words can change parts of speech by adding or changing endings. Adding -*ing* to *summit* changes the noun to a verb. You learned that a mountain's summit is its highest point. What do you think *summiting* means?

---

mentally in a way that involves the mind
persevered continued to try to do something even though it was difficult
ultimate greatest or highest possible

More Information
The Seven Summits are
the highest points on each
of the seven continents:
Kilimanjaro (Africa), Denali
(North America), Elbrus
(Europe), Everest (Asia),
Aconcagua (South
America), Carstenz
(Oceania), and Vinson
(Antarctica).

If she succeeded, she would be the youngest person ever to scale the famed Seven Summits.

Climbing took Danielle's mind off everything else. While she was on a mountain, she could focus on only one thing: getting to the top. "While climbing, I've found myself to be a very different person," she says. "I become very focused and determined. I forget about the pains of blisters, scrapes, bruises, and the fact that I have AD/HD. I just keep on going."

The determination that Danielle learned to show on the mountains began to appear in other areas of her life, such as school and work. "Since I started climbing, the person I am on the mountain has increasingly become the person I am in life. The more time I spend on the mountain, the more that shapes my life and helps me focus down here," Danielle observes. Her dedication can also be seen in the work she did to prepare for her big climbs. Danielle's goal to scale the Seven Summits involved much more than just showing up at each mountain and climbing it.

Mount Everest

Each climb required months of preparation. Not only did Danielle need to keep her climbing skills sharp, but she also needed to raise money for the expensive climbs. Her last pair of climbs, Mount Vinson and Mount Everest, cost about $100,000! To save money, she worked 10-hour days. She also worked to raise money from other sources. She found people who were willing to sponsor her, she gave slide show **presentations** to inform people about her mission, and she sold T-shirts to her supporters.

Finally, Danielle had scaled six of the Seven Summits. She had raised enough money for the seventh. Only Mount Everest stood between her and her goal. On March 28, 2005, Danielle arrived in Katmandu, Nepal, ready to begin the climb.

What's the Main Idea? Which sentence states the main idea of this paragraph? Hint: Make sure that the main idea relates to each detail mentioned in the paragraph.

presentations shows that provide information

This climb presented many of its own challenges. Toward the beginning of the trip, Danielle suffered from **bronchitis,** and later on she battled food poisoning and harsh weather conditions. Danielle admits, "I don't enjoy every moment I am on the mountain, but the energy and excitement of getting to the top keeps me moving." On May 5, she had to work to avoid a dangerous **avalanche.** As she drew closer to the summit, the weather grew colder, and each step became more difficult. But all of Danielle's hard work paid off on June 2, when she finally reached the top.

---

bronchitis a painful swelling of the tubes leading to the lungs
avalanche a large mass of snow, ice, or rock that falls down a slope

Think About It
You can check your understanding by asking yourself questions such as, "Whom is this article about? What did she do? When did she do it? Why?" If you're not sure of the answers, reread the selection until you find the correct information.

Later, Danielle called home to tell her parents that she had succeeded in her goal. Her father told reporters, "She's a pretty excited young lady. She probably could have floated off of Camp Four."

Her mother added, "I'm just proud that she could see this through. It's been something she wanted to do for a long time."

Danielle had many reasons for wanting to scale the Seven Summits. One, of course, was that she simply loves climbing. But Danielle also wanted to show others that people with AD/HD could accomplish great things. She said, "I want to prove to the world what I've always believed: that I can take the lead and get to wherever I want to go in life; that AD/HD will never be able to stop me from living my dream."

How Do Sports Affect Lives?

How has the sport of mountain climbing affected Danielle Fisher's life? Why was her accomplishment so special? What did it prove? What kind of support did Danielle receive in achieving her goal? How much of that support was brought about by Danielle's own effort? What other people do you know who have overcome disabilities to accomplish their goals?

Kids and Extreme Sports

by Kyanna Sutton

Let's say you want to roll down an unpaved hillside on four wheels at top speed. You are not wearing body armor. You have no seat belt, no brakes, and no steering wheel. This is cutting edge. These are extreme sports, where danger and skill equal thrills.

Set a Purpose for Reading
Read to find out what sports are "extreme sports" and why people participate in them.

Find the Details
The main idea of this paragraph is that some kids like extreme sports because they can enjoy them on their own schedule. What details in the paragraph support this idea?

Though **traditional** sports like football, basketball, and hockey aren't exactly going out of style, the world of so-called **extreme** sports keeps growing in popularity. Kids and adults alike are participating in increasing numbers in these risky — if not sometimes downright dangerous — sports. But why?

Some kids are happier riding their skateboards than dealing with the structure of soccer practice. Others like cruising around on their **BMX** bikes until their legs just quit, surfing themselves silly, or spending the entire weekend learning new tricks on their inline skates.

---

traditional handed down over time
extreme far beyond the average
BMX bicycle motocross, a race on a dirt track

For many kids, traditional team sports mean a lot of coaching, rules, pressure, and competition. It's easy to see why some kids are attracted to the individuality and athletic self-expression that are the hallmarks of extreme sports.

Of course, kids are also attracted to extreme sports because they're cool. And who doesn't like being on the cutting edge? Snowboarding, the bad-boy little brother of skiing, was accepted by people who enjoy traditional sports when it became an official Olympic event at the 1998 Nagano Games. Combine the cool factor with better media coverage, and you've got an athletic image that's **rebellious** and brash.

Paul Vail, 29, a BMX freestyle bike-rider since he was 15, balks at the term "extreme sports." "People have been skydiving, skiing, riding bikes, doing tricks, and taking jumps forever. I think the extreme sports label is a gimmick. I like the term **'alternative** sports.'"

Kids in "alternative" sports are expressive, highly skilled athletes. And sports like rock climbing, snowboarding, inline skating, surfing, skateboarding, extreme skiing, and mountain biking (to name just a few) require a great amount of **technical ability** as well as strength and **endurance.**

English Coach
A *hallmark* is "a quality that defines something." What are the hallmarks of extreme sports?

English Coach
A *gimmick* is "a clever device to get your attention." Where do you most often see or hear gimmicks trying to get your attention?

---

rebellious against the normal
alternative different from the ordinary or expected
technical ability skill unique to a certain sport
endurance ability to last for a long time

"Ouch, That Hurts!"

Fear is probably the number-one reason many of us avoid taking risks. For athletes in extreme sports, conquering fear is part of the adventure of sport.

When a skateboarder is practicing tricks on a 15-foot ramp (commonly called a half-pipe), or a mountain biker is flying down a rock-strewn single track trail, and he makes a mistake and falls — well, it's gonna hurt a little. Okay, maybe a lot.

But the athletes I spoke to didn't complain about injuries; in fact, most have enjoyed relatively injury-free experiences in their sports. Brian Krause, a competitive skydiver for the U.S. Army's Golden Knights, has taken thousands of jumps out of airplanes without so much as a sprained ankle.

But Matt Donovan, a pro downhill mountain bike racer from Massachusetts, said that when he first got serious about racing, he had many injuries. "I had two concussions, a separated shoulder, a broken hand, multiple cuts, and tears. And I cracked a rib."

Yes, extreme sports can often lead to extreme injuries. Boys get injured more often than girls, and inline skaters get injured the most. The most common injuries in alternative sports are broken bones, strains, sprains, serious bruising, and facial cuts.

What's the Main Idea?
The main idea of this paragraph is stated clearly. Which sentence tells what the paragraph is mostly about?

But studies show that nearly 75 percent of all people who get injured participating in extreme sports received their injuries because they wore NO protective gear at all!

So, What's the Hype?

Why are more kids and adults flocking to alternative sports? We asked one young extreme athlete why she does what she does. Here's what she had to say.

Kari White: Snowboarder, 14 years old

Q: When did you start snowboarding?
When I was eleven, I pretty much taught myself how to do it.

Q: How did you become interested in snowboarding?
I first tried when I was about ten and hated it because it was so different than skiing, but when my brothers were doing it I had to learn because it looked like so much fun.

Q: How much time do you spend training?
I go to Mammoth Mountain (in California, home of the 2000 Gravity Games) with my brother Shaun on the weekends and it's super fun to ride there.

Q: Do you play other sports?
I play on my high school soccer team, and it helps me stay strong for snowboarding. We practice every day unless we have a game.

Q: Do you get injured in your sport?

The worst I ever got hurt was when I was 'boarding and overshot the landing of a jump and broke my wrist. It was really broken. They had to pop it back in place, and I was too scared to get it numbed by the huge shot, so I just had them do it cold turkey. It hurt really bad!

Q: Why do you think snowboarding has become so popular?

It's just so much fun and I think people like to get away from work and school and enjoy snowboarding in the mountains.

Q: Do you consider snowboarding an extreme sport?

I think snowboarding in the backcountry is really crazy; you have to be really brave. All those **avalanches** and hidden rocks are scary.

Q: Why do you snowboard?

I snowboard because it's really fun and I like learning new tricks and meeting new people.

---

avalanches masses of snow, ice, and rock that fall down slopes

English Coach

Going *cold turkey* is an expression that usually means giving up a habit without the aid of medicine. How did Kari go cold turkey?

Q: What's it like being a female snowboarder?

I think being a female snowboarder is hard because nobody compares you to boys. They just say, "Oh she's good—for a girl!" But there are a lot of girls out there that I look up to because they're charging just like most boys.

Q: Do you find that other girl snowboarders are competitive?

The girls my age at nationals are really competitive, but some are nice. They all have coaches and most don't even go to school. (They have tutors.) I think they take winning really seriously.

Q: Do you compete with the guys?

No, not usually. But it's always fun to free ride with them and race and stuff.

Q: What advice would you give to other girls who want to get into your sport?

Don't be scared, just go out and charge. Don't worry about falling. Ride with a bunch of boys that are going to push you to keep up.

Think About It

You can check your understanding by pausing as you read to ask yourself questions such as, "How does Kari White feel about snowboarding? Why?" If you're not sure of the answer, reread the interview until you find the correct information.

How Do Sports Affect Lives?

What seem to be the main reasons why athletes are drawn to extreme sports? Why do you think extreme sports have become popular? Do you think extreme sports will ever become as popular as tennis or hockey? Why or why not? Have you tried or would you like to try any of the extreme sports mentioned in this selection? Why or why not?

Sports are more than just games to some; they can greatly affect people's lives. The authors of the following essay and poem express strong but very different feelings about sports. Each one describes in painful detail what sports really mean to him.

Right Kick, Wrong Direction

by Joseph Losardo

Set a Purpose for Reading
People play sports for different reasons. Read to find out why this author played sports and what he learned about himself in the process.

I was eleven years old. This was my first soccer game. As the tall, skinny kid stuck in the middle of the muddy field, with little knowledge of the rules and regulations of the game, I was anxious, but still excited. With kids running at me from all directions, I observed the skills that many of my teammates possessed. Their motions appeared to be so smooth and effortless, while their faces revealed their **attachment** to the game. I, on the other hand, lacked the **dedication** that many of the other kids had.

attachment close interest; devotion
dedication devotion to something

This game turned out to be an intense one. My team was trailing behind the entire game, but toward the end, we tied it up. I watched as parents yelled and screamed, filled with excitement and emotion. Many of the parents, with their waving arms and beaming eyes, seemed more involved in the game than their children were.

Suddenly, it was my turn to kick the ball. This was my chance to reveal that I was as good as everyone else. I brought my leg back and was ready to kick with all my strength. I gave a good, hard kick — one of my better ones — but unfortunately, I kicked the ball in the wrong direction. Seeing the disappointed faces of the members of my team, I felt my face go from pale white to bright red. I wanted to run home, faster than I ever ran in a soccer practice.

Over the next few years, I continued to **participate** in a variety of sports. I tried to find the one where I would be the center of attention for the right reasons.

English Coach
When used as a verb, the word *beam* can mean "smile with joy." What does the author mean when he says that many of the parents had "beaming eyes"?

participate to take part in

That never happened. As the firstborn son, my father could not wait to toss the baseball around the backyard with me. Each time he would throw the ball, I somehow managed to trip on a shoelace or stumble over a rock. My father continued to push me, and during my elementary-school years it seemed that I might become quite the athlete. I was able to fake an interest and avoid the action when playing. At the same time, my little brother was suddenly not so little and began to **dominate** the family athletics. His ability and genuine love for sports made me wonder why I was so different.

I began to feel like an outsider, not only with my family, but also with the whole male race. All my friends could play sports, and they all knew of my less-than-perfect abilities. I had many friends to help ease the path of growing up without taking part in sports, but there were still many instances when I was not invited to a football game. It was frustrating to have this inability when **agility** appeared to be such an important aspect of a young child's life.

---

dominate to control or rule over
agility ability to move or do something quickly and easily

Think About It
You can check your understanding by pausing as you read to ask yourself questions, such as, "What made the narrator feel like an outsider?" If you don't know the answer, reread the selection until you find the correct information.

Whenever I was introduced to people, whether it be a kid in school or a friend of a parent, I was always asked if I played basketball — a natural question to a fourteen-year-old six-footer. When I responded "No," everyone told me that I should. But I did not want to, and I was never able to figure out why it mattered so much.

When I became a teenager, I put an end to all my **phoniness** about sports. When my parents finally allowed me to stop participating in Little League and other sports teams, I was filled with mixed emotions. I was happy that I did not have to go through another baseball practice, standing in the outfield, hoping a ball would never be hit in my direction. But on the other hand, I was a "reject." I did not go to basketball practice after school like everyone else. I felt alone.

Eventually, I realized that I was not a **recluse,** but that I enjoyed the company of other people, as well as taking part in activities. I recognized that I was not a social **misfit** but a social butterfly.

Find the Details
The main idea of this paragraph is that the narrator was filled with mixed emotions when he quit playing sports. What details support this idea?

---

phoniness false conduct
recluse a person who is alone, shut away from the world
misfit a person who does not get along well with other people

English Coach
An *aspect* is a part of something. What aspects of your life do you think are most important?

What's the Main Idea?
The author does not tell you directly the main idea of his essay. Use details from what you read and your own experience to tell what you think the main idea is.

New friends helped me to discover my sense of humor, along with my natural **ardor** to explore and appreciate the world around me. I began to focus on the other aspects of my life, the ones I enjoyed. In high school I identified my desire to become a leader, and I involved myself in different student organizations. I also pursued my interests in writing and film. I spent my time being **productive,** but more importantly, I felt good about myself and what I was doing.

My lack of ability for sports was something that separated me from many people, but also made me realize what in life I do enjoy. Now when faced with a challenge, I feel exactly like that little boy who stood, scared and uneasy, in that **intimidating** soccer field. The only difference is that now my uneasiness is accompanied by a surge of confidence in my talent and abilities.

---

ardor strong feeling of warmth or enthusiasm
productive able to make, grow, create
intimidating frightening

Black Hair

by Gary Soto

What Do You Know?
What sport is being described in this poem? What do you know about it?

At eight I was brilliant with my body.

In July, that ring of heat

We all jumped through, I sat in the **bleachers**

Of Romain Playground, in the **lengthening**

Shade that rose from our dirty feet.

The game before us was more than baseball.

It was a figure — Hector Moreno

Quick and hard with turned muscles,

His crouch the one I **assumed** before an **altar**

Of worn baseball cards, in my room.

---

bleachers a section of seats, usually without a roof, where people can watch outdoor sporting events

lengthening getting longer

assumed put oneself in a position

altar a raised table where things of value are displayed

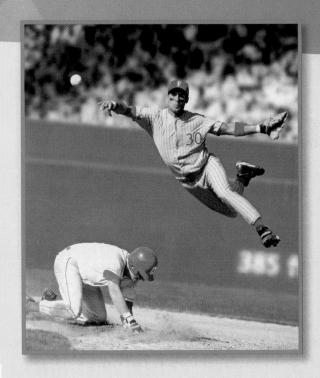

Think About It
Poets often use images, or vivid descriptions, to get their ideas across. What images help you understand how the narrator of this poem feels about baseball?

I came here because I was Mexican, a stick

Of brown light in love with those

Who could do it — the triple and hard slide,

The gloves eating balls into double plays.

What could I do with fifty pounds, my **shyness,**

My black torch of hair, about to go out?

Father was dead, his face no longer

Hanging over the table or our sleep,

And mother was the terror of mouths

Twisting hurt by butter knives.

---

shyness state of being bashful or uncomfortable with other people

28

In the bleachers I was brilliant with my body,
Waving players in and stomping my feet,
Growing sweaty in the **presence** of white shirts.
I chewed sunflower seeds. I drank water
And bit my arm through the late innings.
When Hector lined balls into deep
Center, in my mind I rounded the bases
With him, my face flared, my hair lifting
Beautifully, because we were coming home
To the arms of brown people.

---

presence company

English Coach
When Hector "lined balls into deep center," he hit *line drives*. A *line drive* is a long, straight, hard-hit ball that is difficult to catch. Have you ever seen someone hit a line drive?

How Do Sports Affect Lives?

How did baseball affect the life of the narrator of "Black Hair"? How did the author of "Right Kick, Wrong Direction" feel about sports? What made him quit? How did he make up for his lack of ability in sports? Which attitude as expressed in the essay and the poem is closer to how you feel about sports?

Little League Legend Meets Her Match

Maria Pepe didn't consider herself a girl baseball player. She thought of herself as a good baseball player. But after only three Little League games, she became a pawn in a court fight for the rights of women and girls across the United States.

Maria Pepe was one of the best baseball players in her Hoboken, New Jersey, neighborhood. She hit, pitched, and fielded as well as — if not better than — the local boys. But when the boys joined Little League baseball teams, Pepe was left alone on the **sandlot.** Finally, in 1972, the 11-year-old girl decided to try out for Little League herself. She didn't know then that her experience would change Little League baseball forever.

---

sandlot an empty piece of land often used by young people to play sports

Pepe not only made the team; she made history. She was invited to join the Young **Democrats** and to play alongside the boys. Pepe was thrilled. "I was excited because, for the first time, I'd be able to play in a league where you got to wear a uniform," she remembers. "My folks bought me new **cleats,** and my coach made me the starting pitcher for our opener."

Did she suffer any pre-game jitters? Pepe may have been nervous, but she handled the pressure well. "I wasn't **intimidated** at all, because I had played sandlot ball with and against many of the boys in the league. The only difference between those games and these games was that we wore uniforms and had official **umpires** and coaches."

---

democrats people who believe in government by the people
cleats pieces of metal or plastic fastened to the bottoms of shoes to provide better footing
intimidated worried or frightened
umpires officials who rule on the sports plays

Find the Details
The main idea of this paragraph is that Pepe handled the pressure of her first league game well. What details support this idea?

After only three games, though, Pepe's coach delivered some bad news. When the officials at Little League Headquarters had found out that a girl was playing in the all-boys' baseball league, they were very unhappy. Pepe's coach told her that if she kept playing, the local league would lose its **charter.** That would mean the Little League season would be all over for the local teams before it had hardly begun.

Although Pepe was upset, she knew what choice she had to make. "I didn't want to make a hundred kids mad at me, so I had to step down." She thought that, eventually, she would be allowed back on the team. She had no idea how long that would take.

After stepping down, Pepe became a celebrity of sorts, and the New York Yankees honored her and her family with a special day at Yankee Stadium. The case drew the attention of the media, probably because of Hoboken's **proximity** to New York City.

charter an official paper that gives an organization the right to perform
proximity the state of being close or near

Maria Pepe and her mother share honors received for her contribution to sports.

That, in turn, drew the attention of the National Organization for Women (NOW).

"The newspapers were all doing stories about it, and then my parents got a call from NOW," Pepe recalled. "They asked my parents if they (NOW) could represent me in a case that could get Little League to admit girls. It shocked my folks that I even wanted to play baseball . . . [but] my folks finally decided to let NOW go ahead."

The case dragged on for more than two years, as did similar cases around the United States.

"I can remember coming home every day from school, asking my mom if they made a decision," Pepe said. "I didn't understand at the time what was taking so long. Of course, by the time it was decided, I was in high school and too old for Little League."

The door closed on Pepe's Little League career, but it opened wide for the careers of millions of girls. The final ruling came in early 1974, when local Little Leagues in New Jersey were told they must allow girls to try out. Instead of resisting further, Little League decided to admit girls worldwide.

More Information
NOW is one of the largest groups in the United States devoted to making things equal between women and men. Why do you think NOW wanted to help Maria Pepe?

The court's ruling made headline news across the country.

Edwardsville Intelligencer

I on Sports

New Jersey Allows Girl Little Leaguers

Since the ruling in 1974, millions of girls have played on Little League baseball and softball teams. Some are, as Maria Pepe was, the only girl on their teams; others play on all-girl teams. Today, the Little Leagues **boast** nearly 500,000 female players.

One of these female players, Katie Brownell, recently made history of her own. On May 14, 2005, the 12-year-old was the first girl in the history of Little League baseball to pitch a no-hitter. The 18 batters Brownell faced simply couldn't hit her curveballs, changeups, and fastballs.

Katie was honored on July 7, 2005, in a ceremony at the National Baseball Hall of Fame. She donated her Little League Dodgers uniform and spoke shyly to a crowd of 300. In her speech, she made sure to thank God, her parents, the Little League, her fans — and Maria Pepe.

---

boast to take pride in having or doing something

English Coach

Curveballs, changeups, and fastballs are kinds of pitches that a pitcher throws to make a batter swing and miss. Curveballs move in a curve and fastballs move fast. What do you think a changeup is?

Katie Brownell and Maria Pepe celebrate at the National Baseball Hall of Fame on July 7, 2005.

Pepe was present for the speech and congratulated Brownell on her **achievement.** The former and present Little League players, over thirty years apart in age, both delighted in the celebration. They posed for photographs together, and Brownell signed autographs for her fans. "I can't tell you how thrilled I was when I heard what Katie had accomplished," said Pepe. "When the story broke, I had numerous friends and relatives e-mail it to me. That was my dream as a kid. I wanted to do something on the diamond like Katie did — something rare and **inspirational.**"

Pepe is thankful for her Little League experience, despite never having the chance to throw a no-hitter. She reflected, "I feel good inside about what happened, even though I only got to play three games. I think the experience made me a different person, a stronger person."

---

achievement success, act of reaching a goal
inspirational able to fill others with a desire to do something

Think About It
Why do you think many of Pepe's friends and relatives e-mailed her the story of Katie Brownell? If you're not sure of the answer, reread the selection until you find the correct information.

35

Pepe is happy with the way things turned out. "I always felt like, someday, this was all going to come full circle. It was never my way to reach out to anyone, but just to talk to people who came to me about it, if they wanted to. I was just a shy kid who wanted to play baseball."

Few people have the opportunity to see their actions change history so dramatically in their lifetimes. "The interesting thing is that I never scripted it this way," Pepe said. "I had no desire to cause a **ruckus** or become some sort of historical figure. I just wanted to play ball."

Far from bitter about her three-game career, Maria Pepe looks forward to a bright future: "I get to play forever in the girls that come after me."

---

ruckus uproar

English Coach
Many English words can be used in different ways. The noun *script* means "the written form of a story." When Pepe says that she "never scripted it this way," she uses *script* as a verb. She means that she did not plan for the story of her life to turn out the way it did.

How Do Sports Affect Lives?

What big changes happened in the Little League in 1974? How have the changes affected the game since then? Why do you think girls were not allowed to play in the Little League before 1974? Do you think girls would still not be allowed to play in Little League if Maria Pepe had not joined a team? Do you think there are some sports that should be played only by boys or only by girls? Explain your answer.

How Can Music Make a Difference?

Music is everywhere. It reaches us from radios, elevators, and TVs. We spin disks, shuffle tracks, and download files. We sing and we play instruments, creating our own sounds. Music brings us together and sets us apart. Through music we express ourselves in a deeply personal way.

The selections in this unit show how music can make a difference in our lives. You will see how music affects race relations and public relations — and can build a bridge to better human relations.

Hip-Hop Heaven

Music, like all other forms of art, never stays the same for very long. Music styles change when someone starts a new kind of expression, and it becomes popular. Hip-hop grew in this way. This selection tells about the beginning of hip-hop, the people who helped it grow, and the ways it has changed.

English Coach

A cultural awakening is a change in the arts, beliefs, or customs of a society. The society "wakes up" to a change in the way things are seen or appreciated. Can you think of any other cultural awakenings?

Hip-hop is a movement, a **cultural** awakening, a voice of a generation. It is the beat that found its rhythm in New York City and then boomed and howled across the nation and around the world.

The roots of hip-hop can be traced all the way back to ancient West Africa. In those days, storytellers called *griots* used their voices and drums to create a musical sound very much like today's hip-hop.

---

cultural of the arts, beliefs, and customs of a people or group

Some of these traditions came to the New World when slaves were brought over to America.

Like most musical traditions, though, hip-hop came about because of several **factors.** In Jamaica in the 1960s a form of music called *dub* became very popular. Many people believe dub was the most direct influence on what later became hip-hop. Dub musicians were called *DJs* (short for disc jockeys) because they used existing records to make their music. They took recordings of popular Jamaican music called *reggae* and added sound effects. Recording one set of sounds on top of another is called *dubbing.* Along with the music, listeners might hear animal noises, babies crying, and even **producers** shouting to the musicians.

factors things that help bring about a certain result

producers people who manage the making of an album, movie, show, or other kind of entertainment

More Information
Reggae music started in Jamaica during the 1960s. It was based on both traditional African music and the rhythm and blues music played in New Orleans, Louisiana. Bob Marley was a well-known reggae musician. Do you know of any others?

When dub DJs made their recordings, they repeated certain parts over and over. They called these repeated parts *breaks*. Breaks were usually quite short with a heavy beat.

In 1967, Jamaican immigrants brought dub to the United States. One of them was Kool Herc. He had been born Clive Campbell in Kingston, Jamaica. But he moved to the United States when he was thirteen. As a young man growing up in the Bronx area of New York City, Herc played his music in the streets and later in music clubs. He spun reggae records and recited rhymes he made up on the spot. People were interested in what he was doing. But most of them weren't fans of reggae music. So Herc started using funk, rock, and disco records instead.

Kool Herc in 2004

Using what he'd learned playing dub, Herc found a way to mix the sounds of two records at the same time. He would take two copies of the same record and use a machine called an *audio mixer* to jump back and forth between them. In this way, he could play one short section, or break, of the song as many times as he wanted. Each break had a very strong beat. This made the music easy to dance to. He used a pair of record **turntables** as a kind of musical instrument. In this way, he used other people's music to make new music. This later became known as "found sound." Soon other ways of mixing sound developed, and hip-hop was born.

Herc wanted to make a name for himself. He wanted to make sure the music he played wouldn't be just like any other DJ's sound. So he tried to find records that no one else would have. He went to shops that sold rare records. "This is where your **recognition,** your rep, comes from," he later said. "You have to have a record nobody else has got, or you're the first one to have it. You've got to be the first, can't be the second."

Compare and Contrast
Herc spun records and recited rhymes he made up on the spot. How was what Herc did similar to what dub musicians did? How was it different?

English Coach
A *name* is "the word or words a person is called by." *Name* can also mean "a reputation." Which type of name did Herc want?

audio having to do with sound or hearing
turntables devices used for playing records
recognition attention or praise

Herc's music began to bring in large crowds. Soon he was hosting all-night dance parties and working in large music clubs. Often he made up rhymes that contained popular phrases and the **slang** of the day. Sometimes the rhymes had to do with people he knew in the audience. "Davey D is in the house," he would chant over the loud, thumping music. "And he'll turn it out without a doubt." The words didn't always make sense, but the crowds loved it. Sometimes people would shout out there their own names in the hope that Herc might mention them.

English Coach
The slang expression *in the house* means "here, in this place." *Turn it out* means "to show what you can do" as in dance, sing, or perform.

---

slang the casual language of a certain group or people

42

As Herc became more popular, he decided to focus all his attention on being a DJ. He got two friends to take over at the microphone while he spun records and mixed the sound. This new focus made it easy for him to create a new, more **complex** sound.

As the hip-hop **trend** caught on, more performers started taking part. Like DJ Kool Herc, they talked to the audience in rhyme while the music played. Originally these performers were called *MCs* (short for master of ceremonies). Later they became known as *rappers*. Early rappers didn't do much more than introduce themselves and lead a simple spoken chorus over the recorded music. But as time went on, rappers got more creative. They started using humor and more complex rhymes. They had contests, called *battles,* to see who was the best rapper. Sometimes these contests took place in music clubs. But sometimes two rappers simply faced off on a street corner and tried to **outdo** each other with clever rhymes and insults. Confidence and **creativity** were the most important things a performer could have. The audiences got to decide the winners.

complex having many different connected or related parts
trend a popular direction or movement
outdo to do better than
creativity the quality of being able to make new and original things

Summarize It
In your own words, summarize how rappers have changed over time. Remember to include only the most important details in your summary.

Think About It
Why would confidence and creativity be the most important things a rapper could have? If you're not sure of the answer, reread the selection until you find the correct information.

43

Rapping gave young people a chance to express themselves. The music didn't have a lot of rules. No one had to take lessons to do it. It was the kind of performing just about anyone could practice. All a rapper had to do was be original and keep the beat. But rapping also showed off each performer's personality.

In the late 1970s, a new form of dance became an important part of hip-hop culture. Break dancing began in the South Bronx of New York. This type of dance was very athletic. Its moves included kicks, flips, and spins. As hip-hop music played, crowds of people would form around a dancer who would stun them by spinning around for long periods . . . on his head!

Make Inferences
A new form of dance, *break dancing,* came about because of hip-hop. How does the name of this dance form relate to the origins of hip-hop?

By the end of the 1970s hip-hop music had become very popular. It had spread throughout the United States. From there, it had spread all over the world. It had become the music of the new generation, a street music that crossed borders and cultures.

How Can Music Make a Difference?

Has the music style created by Kool Herc made a difference in American culture? How? How has hip-hop changed since it began? Do you think hip-hop will continue to change? If so, how will it change?

Striving to Make Music Under the Streets of NYC

by Daniel Strieff and Jon Sweeney, MSNBC

When was the last time you attended a music performance? Last week? Last month? People who take the subway in New York City attend at least one a day. Some very good musicians are brightening people's lives by taking their music underground.

Straining to make his music heard over the roar of trains far below the traffic-clogged streets of Manhattan, singer-songwriter Theo Eastwind is a long way from the bright lights of the big-time music business. That's just fine with him.

"I'm not in it for any big money or anything. "[If] you have a talent, if you have a **passion,** then you can still come down here and you can still do it," he said. "Not because you're going to be rich.

Compare and Contrast
Think about what Theo Eastwind says about being a subway musician. As you read, compare Eastwind's feelings to those of the other musicians. How are they alike and different?

---

passion strong liking for an activity

Theo Eastwind

Not because you're going to be a superstar. . . .
It's because you wanna do it."

Eastwind is one of more than 100 official subway musicians performing in at least 25 locations throughout the 468-station New York subway system. Musicians have been playing the New York subway system for decades. But a program was established in 1987 to spruce up the city's subway stations and make travelers' journeys more enjoyable. Each spring, a panel of judges determines which acts are accepted into the program.

"This gives them a way to be organized, and it gives them a space to play so that they're not fighting for a little corner," a Music Under New York spokeswoman said.

Think About It
Have you ever heard a street musician perform? Do you think New York's program for choosing official subway musicians is a good idea? Why or why not?

47

More Information
New York City is often called "The Big Apple." Many other U.S. cities have nicknames too, and some of them have more than one. What nicknames for other cities do you know?

For many tourists in the Big Apple, subway musicians add **local color** to what can be a frustrating attempt to get around the city's transit system. For New Yorkers, live tunes can make their stuffy travels a little more pleasant.

A modern-day "troubadour"

Eastwind turned to performing underground when the bakery he worked at closed. He now regularly plays throughout the subway system, on the street, and in local clubs. With a wispy goatee, well-worn T-shirt, and light hair peaking out from beneath a battered cap, he looks — and acts — the part of a street musician perfectly. On a recent afternoon at 68th Street-Hunter College Station, his open guitar case collecting money in front of him, Eastwind thought about his role as a musician.

"I would say that underground musicians, or even street musicians generally [are] a continuation of the culture of troubadours," he said.

---

local color behavior, speech, or style that belongs to a certain place or time

troubadour a traveling musician from the Middle Ages who composed and sang songs and poems

48

But musicians playing to the nearly 3 million daily **commuters** on New York's subway face a special set of challenges.

"Playing in the subways is so difficult because you have people who didn't come down here to see you; they want to catch the train," Eastwind said. "And to catch them, you've got a window of maybe 10–20 seconds to get someone's interest, and then if there's no train, to keep their interest. . . . You've gotta shape yourself around what people like."

Summarize It
In your own words, summarize the challenges subway musicians face. Look for details in the second paragraph to help you.

---

commuters people who travel between home and work or school

Musically diverse

Arts are nothing new in New York's subway. The system's Arts for Transit program tries to bring arts exhibitions into the underground. Recently, a mural by world-**renowned** artist Roy Lichtenstein was unveiled at the 42nd Street Station. Heru Ptah began selling his first novel on the subway. An MTV Books director bought a copy while riding the A train in February 2003 and convinced MTV to buy the rights to it. But the variety of musicians playing under the streets of New York makes it perhaps one of the most **vibrant** performance spaces in the country.

---

diverse having several or many different kinds
renowned widely honored or respected
vibrant full of energy

More Information
Roy Lichtenstein was an artist who painted images from popular culture, such as comics. Heru Ptah sold more than 8,000 copies of his book, *A Hip Hop Story,* on the subways of New York City and through his Web site.

While some musicians, like Eastwind, seem perfectly happy playing underground, others see it as a stepping stone. And still others do it just to make ends meet. The Susan Cagle Band, which describes its sound as "ethnic rock" — mixing pop and light rock with a **Caribbean** style — has set its sights high. Set up at Union Square Station recently, the band attracted a crowd of travelers who took the time to stop, sign up to the group's e-mail lists, and listen.

"We often have people come up to us and say, 'Well, I've known you and seen you play since you were this high,'" Susan said as she signaled waist-height. "[But] as much as the subway is a part of us, because we've sung in the subway so much, it would be a big breath of relief when the day comes when we don't have to play in the subway anymore."

The band, which also plays local clubs and hopes to release a second album soon, has settled here after years on the road. Susan says the group's subway dates are the key to building a fan base from which it can build to wider success.

Caribbean   of the Caribbean Sea and its islands, located between North America and South America

English Coach
The authors state that some musicians see playing in the subway as a "stepping stone." Here, a *stepping stone* is "a way to advance to something greater." What do you think the subway artists hope to gain?

Make Inferences
The article says that the band has settled here after years on the road. Where is "here"— in the subway or in New York City? Why do you think that?

Lorenzo La Roc

"It's the best **venue** for getting heard," she said. "Also, it's good practice. . . . If you can play in the subway and get a crowd and be successful, you can play pretty much anywhere."

An "electric violinist" at Penn Station

Lorenzo La Roc, one of New York's few electric violinists, is tough to miss. La Roc is a mover. His musical performance is balanced by his dancing and light sidestepping of commuters. Though the crowded and stuffy station seemed a far from **ideal** venue, La Roc clearly **relished** the audience.

"You've got a million people walking by you," he said. "This is as live as it gets." La Roc said he has been playing the subway system for 15 years. "It's hard work, but it's a great living if you're doing it right and [well,]" La Roc said as he wiped sweat from his brow.

---

venue the place where an action or event happens
ideal perfect or excellent
relished took great pleasure in

He is proud of his local roots and their effect on his music. "You know, it's New York City and I'm a New Yorker, if you give New Yorkers what they want, they'll [understand] it," La Roc said. "You know, you can't fool somebody here. They either like it or don't."

And commuters at 42nd Street Station seem to like **accordionist** Mitu Busioc. He's not as flashy as some of the other underground musicians. But Busioc clearly **relishes** his time playing "music popular/music international" to travelers, even with the hustle and bustle around him. The subway gives him an ideal space for him to entertain, day after day, in a public space, he said. And why does he play underground?

"Because I have five kids," Busioc said with a broad smile.

---

accordionist a person who plays an accordion, or hand-held organ
relishes enjoys; gets much pleasure from

English Coach
Roots are the feelings of loyalty that tie a person to a place. La Roc is proud of his *local roots*. What place is La Roc tied to?

Think About It
What do Busioc's children have to do with his playing underground? If you're not sure, look back over the information until you find the correct answer.

How Can Music Make a Difference?

In what way can music make a difference for subway travelers? How does playing in the subway make a difference for some of the musicians? Do you listen to music as you travel to and from school? Would it make a difference to you if the music you heard in the subway was live or recorded? Why?

Ev'ry Time I Feel the Spirit

by David Barr III

Marian Anderson was a singer who experienced success throughout Europe long before the American public accepted her. In this scene from the play, Anderson takes a singing lesson and also learns why the music she makes can make a difference in the world.

Make Inferences
From Boghetti's comments, what do you think Marian was doing wrong that made Boghetti stop her and give instruction?

Scene 8

(Lights up on Boghetti and the young student Marian Anderson in Boghetti's studio. Marian is singing a song from an opera in German.)

BOGHETTI: Come now Miss Anderson. *Boldness of attack*. The notes come first, then the **interpretation** comes on top of them afterwards.

MARIAN: But I. . . .

BOGHETTI: Ahhhhh . . . I am the teacher, and you are the student. Again, from the top of the song. Notes first. Interpretation comes on top.

---

interpretation the way an artist performs or presents a work of art

MARIAN: On top, yes . . . notes first . . . interpretation on top. Yes, of course. *(She sings again.)*

BOGHETTI: *Stop!* Your breathing **techniques** are terrible. For nearly *two* years we have discussed this. In the middle of the scale, you just breathe and sing. You forget all about *technique.* Marian, you *must* be able to sing up and down the scale with no change in quality of tone. From highest to lowest. You also need to work on your **pianissimo.**

MARIAN: *I do?*

BOGHETTI *(warm chuckle, shaking his head)*: *Yes, you do.* The *softer* areas of your voice. The more quiet tones within your singing voice that I know you possess. So for now, pay strict attention to what's on the page in front of you.

MARIAN: Yes. The notes are on the page but not the feeling, and the emotion. That's . . . that's . . . what I *feel . . . inside. . . .*

English Coach
A *scale* is made up of eight musical notes. As you sing up the scale, the notes get higher. They become lower as you sing down the scale. Do you know of any other kind of scale?

---

techniques methods or style of doing something
pianissimo soft or quiet playing or singing

BOGHETTI: Precisely. But, when you are first learning voice, you must **sacrifice** emotion. You must have technique. Technique is the key in the beginning, then the feeling will follow. It's all a question of balance.

(Boghetti goes to his Victrola and puts on a record, Wagner's "Tristan and Isolde." Music swells as Marian and Boghetti listen.)

Music is a faith, Miss Anderson. You must feel like you are an adventurer, not by choice but by fate. You must **immerse** yourself in the development of your voice. There can be no room or time for **infidelity** in these studies. Your voice is your husband. It is your soul mate for life. You must marry it. . . . You hold tightly to it because it gives your life a meaning that nothing else — nothing in this world at least — can possibly provide. Yes?

Summarize It
Think about the most important ideas in the first paragraph. How would you retell Boghetti's statement in your own words?

sacrifice to give something up to achieve a goal
Victrola a brand of early record player
immerse to absorb
infidelity not being faithful or loyal

Marian Anderson performing on the steps of the Lincoln Memorial on April 9, 1939

MARIAN: I think so.

BOGHETTI: Thus . . . you must look at our rehearsals as an artistic training ground. The concerts are a *battleground*, Miss Anderson. And your *voice* is the weapon. A musical instrument to use in battle. Yes?

MARIAN: Yes.

BOGHETTI: Good. Now we must rest for a moment. *(pauses, looking at Marian)* Marian, I must tell you that *music* can be a dreadful thing.

MARIAN *(confused and amused, trying to see if this is yet another test)*: What?

BOGHETTI: I have created and played music all of my life, and yet I still do not know if I truly understand it. Let me ask you . . . what does music do for you?

MARIAN: I . . . I don't think I completely understand the question.

BOGHETTI: What does *music* itself do *for* you?

MARIAN: It . . . **enriches** my spirit, I suppose.

Compare and Contrast
Boghetti compares Marian's voice to a weapon. Why does he make this comparison? How will this comparison help Marian?

---

enriches makes better or richer

Think About It

Boghetti says that the secret of music lies "in its ability to transport one directly into the mind and soul of the composer." What does he mean by this? How does it affect the way a singer should sing?

BOGHETTI (*slight chuckle*): *Enriches your spirit?* Nonsense. If you hear a marching band at a baseball game is your spirit *enriched?* No . . . you simply cheer on **cue.** No, Marian, I believe that the secret of music is much more complicated than simple enrichment of the spirit. I believe that its secret lies in its ability to transport one directly into the *mind* and *soul* of the composer. So . . . what do you think was in the composer's soul when he wrote this, the final **aria** for his **heroine** *Isolde?*

MARIAN: I couldn't really say.

BOGHETTI: But you have sung this selection in recitals. Don't you *know* what you are singing?

MARIAN (*slightly embarrassed*): Well, not word for word. But . . .

---

cue a signal to begin a speech or action
aria a song written for one singer
heroine the main female character in a work of art

Eleanor Roosevelt presents Marian Anderson with the Spingarn Medal of the National Association for the Advancement of Colored People in 1939.

BOGHETTI *(slightly annoyed at her response; mumbling)*: Of course.

MARIAN: I know what the song is about. That is, I know the story. But I confess, I . . .

BOGHETTI: That's not enough. Not enough. *(sternly turns the record off; long pause)* You must learn the meaning if you are to do the aria justice. *(restarts the Victrola; music of Isolde's aria swells)* A woman . . . not just any woman . . . but a *sorceress* . . . is trying to reach her lover. He lies helpless on his sick bed with a life-threatening fever. She waits for him, tired and alone. Then the woman is physically carried away by the music . . . *transported*. And when she finally reaches him, she dies, collapsing over her lover's dead body. This is what Wagner was trying to communicate to the listener. Nothing but music can make one feel these things. *(Marian is still lost in the music.)* Can you feel her pain?

MARIAN *(transported)*: Yes.

---

sorceress a female worker of magic

transported moved to express or experience strong emotions or feelings

Make Inferences
Why do you think Boghetti is annoyed with Marian for not knowing what she is singing?

BOGHETTI: Good. There is no shortcut. To sing certain German songs and older Italian songs, you must *first* understand the how and the why of what you are doing. Then you must be prepared for the problems you may face when you perform in certain places.

MARIAN *(confused)*: What problems?

BOGHETTI: Marian, listen. Some who come to hear you sing may simply hate you because of your *color*.

MARIAN: No.

BOGHETTI: Yes my child, it is true. And they will hate you for being as good as any white singer who performs songs. For maybe even being better than any white woman who performs these songs. They are afraid of you because they cannot laugh at you and make fun of you as if you were simply singing those — what do they call them in America? — mammy songs. These are the kind of songs they are used to seeing ALL Negroes do on the New York stage. Most of America doesn't understand or simply doesn't want to hear a Negro singing beautiful music.

More Information

Marian Anderson was born in 1902. She won first prize in the New York Philharmonic voice competition in 1925, but at the time African-American singers were not invited to perform on the concert stage.

Marian Anderson at the Department of Interior Auditorium for the dedication of a mural commemorating her concert at the Lincoln Memorial, January 6, 1943

They are used to seeing Negroes in entirely different roles when they come to the theater. And there are many, many other **obstacles** like these that might block your path.

MARIAN: What other obstacles?

BOGHETTI: Obstacles that will have you questioning your own self-worth and purpose. But you will perform for them *all* one day on the world's finest stages. And you will show them how it can be.

MARIAN *(pause; then determined)*: Yes. But not before I am absolutely sure that I am ready, and that I am good enough for them — or for anybody — anywhere in the world.

(Lights fade on scene.)

---

obstacles things that stop or stand in the way of someone's goal

What Do You Know?
Think about what you know about life for African Americans before and after the civil rights movement. What obstacles might Marian Anderson have faced?

How Can Music Make a Difference?
Marian Anderson became the first African American to perform as a regular member of the New York Metropolitan Opera. How do you think Marian Anderson's success made a difference in the lives of African Americans at that time? Do you agree that a great singer must know not just the music but also the meaning behind the music? Why? Do you think a person who does not sing opera can be a great singer? Explain your answer.

The Song of Stones River

by Jennifer Armstrong

The War Between the States lasted four years and claimed more than 600,000 lives. On both sides, many of the soldiers were under the age of 16; the youngest soldiers were the drummer boys. Music can make a difference in war — but in more ways than one.

What Do You Know?
The War Between the States, or the American Civil War, divided our nation in two. How was the nation divided?

By July of 1862, the War Between the States had already torn fifteen months off the calendar. Our boys had fought bloodily in the battlefields of Virginia and on the other side of the Appalachians, too, in Tennessee, Kentucky, and Missouri. With all the cards against them — fewer men, fewer guns, fewer supplies of all kinds — the **rebel** army of the **Confederacy** had won battle after battle.

---

rebel a person who resists a law, custom, or government
Confederacy the government formed by the Southern states during the Civil War

62

Our powerful army of the United States was getting kicked all over the map. The Rebels were beating us **Yankees.**

Over in Murfreesboro, Tennessee, Federal troops were looking to hold control of the railroad lines so the supply trains could come through from Kentucky with food for men, horses, and mules. Like a summer storm, Confederate **cavalry** crashed down upon them, and forced a surrender. The way was now clear for the Rebels to invade northward.

And northward they ran, into Kentucky, hastening upward toward Ohio like a burning fuse. My brother was in a **Union regiment** at Green River Bridge in September when the advancing Confederate army broke upon them and forced another surrender. The defeated boys of the Union **garrison** were made prisoners of war, my brother among them.

Make Inferences
Think about what you know of transportation in the 1800s. Why was it important for the Federal troops to keep control of the railroad lines?

A Yankee soldier offers water to a wounded Confederate soldier.

Yankees Union soldiers in the Civil War
cavalry troops trained to fight on horseback
Union regiment a unit of Union soldiers
garrison a military post or fort

A drummer boy

Now more divisions of the Union army, and me and my drum with them, had to trudge south along the rail lines to beat back the Confederate invasion of Kentucky. By early October, the drought had burned the ground coal-hard, and we were worn to a thread before we'd even met the Rebels. Me beating **cadence** on my drum was the only beating going on at that warm time. From north and from south, footsore soldiers marched under a blistering sun. We shook the last drops of water from our canteens; the bugler was too dry to blow his horn.

We came upon a creek in Perryville, with a unit of Arkansas soldiers refreshing themselves in the shade, and this lit off a huge battle that ended with victory for us at last. By nightfall the **scorched** Confederates were retreating back toward the Cumberland Gap, back into Tennessee. The summer **campaign** had beaten us all as dry and thin as leather straps, and the weary Confederate troops were looking forward to settling in for their winter camp and singing restful songs.

English Coach
Words often have more than one meaning. The word *beating* can mean "striking or hitting something to make a sound," or "defeating someone in battle." Which meaning is used in the phrase "Me beating cadence on my drum…"?

---

cadence   the beat of music
scorched   burned and dried out by the heat
campaign   a military plan of action

But we were on our way to the Cumberland Gap, too. Throughout the fall, I drummed us after the retreating Rebels, southward across the mountains into east Tennessee, and then dogged them west on the road to Nashville. Autumn's crops lay forgotten in the fields — pumpkins and apples abuzz with yellow jackets while the people in the countryside tried to keep out of the way of us bluecoats. When late December's darkness closed in around us, we and the Confederates both were camped outside Murfreesboro, Tennessee, in the rocky cedar **glades** along the banks of the narrow Stones River.

What's the Sequence?
This story is told in time order. What words in this paragraph help you know when things are happening?

The Battle of Stones River

There would be another battle. Not a man among us doubted it. Even though the summer and fall had been one long weary march broken up with bitter fighting, and even though it was Christmas, there would be no rest for us. In our camp, men wrote letters to their wives and mothers as they crouched near the cook-fires. And I knew that the Confederate boys were doing the same over where they lay, in their **bivouacs** on the cold limestone.

---

glades open spaces in a forest or group of trees
bivouacs camps put up by soldiers

In the rope corrals, the bony mules who pulled our baggage wagons **brayed** their complaints into the darkness. It seemed to me that I could let out just as **desolate** a cry without much effort.

Christmas came, and with it came heartache and lonesomeness. The chill breeze brought tears to my eyes. Or maybe it was thoughts of home — my ma, my little sisters. I'd been so proud to show off my drum and rattle the sticks for them. I did not know music could lead me to such a place.

Why am I here? I wondered as I thought of my home, my dog, and my companions. What is this war for? From each encampment, the spark and flash of campfires were visible. Tomorrow, the spark and flash would be **artillery** blasts and musket fire, and winter sunlight would glitter on **bayonets.** From each encampment, the low murmur of voices mingled with the mutter of water over stones. Tomorrow, the stones would resound with the **din and discord** of shots and screams, and I would play the cadence that drove men forward into death.

---

brayed made a loud, harsh cry
desolate lonely and sad
artillery large, mounted guns that are too big to carry
bayonets knives attached to the noses of rifles for use in close fighting
din and discord musical tones that together are harsh and unpleasant

Make Inferences
How have the drummer boy's feelings changed since the start of the war? Which lines in this paragraph and the next one support your answer?

Compare and Contrast
The author compares and contrasts Christmas night to what the next day will bring. How does this help you understand the drummer boy's feelings? How are his feelings about the two days different?

To raise our spirits, the regimental band began to play. Our fellows let loose with "Yankee Doodle," and it rang like metal in the frosty air. I blew on my fingers to warm them before I could get a proper grasp on the drumsticks.

The Battle of Murfreesboro

Then we heard a band on the rebel side strike up "Dixie," vying to drown us out.

Our boys hollered to our band to play "The Star-Spangled Banner," and in between the **bars** our ears caught the strains of "Bonnie Blue Flag."

Back and forth we fought with songs, firing ourselves into the kind of hot excitement a man needs to carry him into deadly battle. The fellows grabbed their muskets by the hand, as if they was their sweethearts at a square dance, and breathed hard and remembered the fights they'd already seen and the lead they'd already let fly.

But then, in a lull, one of the bands — and I can't say which side it come from — began a quieter tune, and all around me the fellows felt their hearts catch in their throats. I lowered my drum. The words of the familiar song came to our lips, where moments before we had been thirsty for battle cries.

What Do You Know?
The author describes a different battle — a musical one — as the troops fight with songs. Have you ever had a similar experience? What was it?

bars sections of music

"Mid pleasures and palaces though I may roam,
Be it ever so humble, there's no place like home!"

The tender words rose into the air with the sparks of the campfires on both sides, and our hearts were soothed and **gentled.** *"Home!"* we sang, all of us, Yankee and Rebel alike. *"Home! Sweet, sweet home! There's no place like home!"* If there is a sweeter tune, it has not been sung for living ears.

When the sun arose, the dread war would start **anew,** but for that moment in Tennessee we were all just Americans, singing in harmony, and our country was whole again.

---

gentled made soft and peaceful
anew over again

Summarize It
In your own words, summarize the battle of the songs and how it ended.

How Can Music Make a Difference?

What difference does music make in this story? Do you think the soldiers were aware that they had begun fighting with songs instead of with weapons? Why? Why was one song able to unite the soldiers from different armies? Do you think this event really happened? Could it happen? Why or why not?

Unit 3

What Makes a Good Friend?

There are many different types of friends. Some we don't know well, but we enjoy spending time with them. Others are as close as family members, and we depend on them every day.

The selections in this unit are all about friends. Yet each friend and friendship is unique. As you read, think about what is important to these friends. Then ask yourself, what is important to me? What makes a good friend?

Leaving 'El Combito'

I lost my truest friends when I moved to the U.S.

by Angy Gonzalez

How would you feel if you, or a close friend, suddenly had to move away? When Angy Gonzalez finds out she will have to say goodbye to her "combito," she knows her life will never be the same.

The day I left Colombia for the United States, I was thinking every second about my friends. I hadn't said goodbye to them — I couldn't bear to.

Standing in the airport at age 12, it was as if I had a photo of **"el combito"** (that's what we called ourselves) in my empty hand. A picture of a bunch of noisy kids growing together, not only physically but **mentally** — experimenting with new things together, watching each others' backs, covering each others' mistakes, talking to one another like family.

"el combito" Spanish for "the combo," a name for a meal that combines several different foods

mentally in the mind

English Coach
One meaning of the word *watch* is "to take care of" or "to keep safe." What do you think *watching each others' backs* means?

70

I saw myself vanishing from that picture, and then gone. I felt such a deep sadness that day. Even if I were leaving today, almost five years later, I don't think I could say goodbye.

We Fit Like 'El Combito'

My "combito" were my friends during 6th and part of 7th grade. We had all our classes together and were always talking and making jokes during class. Maribel, who looked older than the rest of us, was my closest friend, Pilar was short but very **aggressive,** and Angelica was a starter in basketball. Fernanda was the youngest, and Paola was the friendly but sad one. Last but not least was me, the sweet but noisy girl.

We came up with thousands of lame names for our group, like "white witches" and "mean freshmen" *(las odiosas primiparas)*, but we stuck with "el combito." We used to eat all the junky food we could afford, and we'd always order the combo (el combito), which had six things: soda, French fries, hamburger, hot dog, special salsa, and dessert.

---

aggressive quick to take action

Visualize It
Use the descriptions in this paragraph to imagine what Angy's friends looked like. Can you picture them in your mind?

71

Think About It
Why did the friends call themselves "el combito"? What should you do if you don't understand why they chose this name?

Since we were initially a group of six girls who fit together like the combo, we started calling ourselves "el combito." Separately, we were six unique girls, but together we formed a magic and rare flavor. In the middle of 6th grade Diana became the seventh girl to join us. Later, guys started joining too — Freddie, a metal fan, and Francisco, the cutest guy at school.

A World Rich in Trust

This was my first time in public school. I think I became especially close to my new friends because they seemed more real than my old private school friends, most of whom were wealthy and never had to work for anything.

English Coach
Richer can mean "having more money" or "having or producing more of something." Which meaning of *richer* is used here? How does it apply to Angy's friends?

My new friends opened me up to a world richer in trust and understanding. We listened to and supported each other.

Maribel helped me realize it was better for me to stay with my mom instead of moving in with my father and stepmother. When Angelica and Diana talked about how badly their fathers treated them, Francisco encouraged them to break free from their **abusive** homes.

---

abusive   treating others badly

Freddie shared his dreams of someday going to college and traveling to other continents. And when Paola didn't have enough money for lunch or simply to get to school, we pooled our money to help her.

'I'm Moving Forever'

I felt so peaceful and secure to have friends who cared about my feelings and gave me advice. Nowadays I have friends who kind of listen, but most of the time I feel I'm the one giving advice instead of receiving it.

"El combito" taught me the meaning of real friendship — having people you can truly trust, who care about you and won't spread your secrets around, and who are always there, even when they're not physically present. You can have as many acquaintances as you can count, but real friends you can count within your two hands.

The first time I told "el combito" I was leaving, they thought it was only for vacation. Later I told them, "I'm moving forever."

Compare and Contrast
Reread the comparison between Angy's "el combito" friends and her new friends. How are her new friends different from her old ones?

'We'll Sing Our Song for You'

My friends were happy for me, since in Colombia the United States seems like the land of opportunity. But then Maribel started crying and said, "Now who am I going to talk to?" That made me feel like the worst friend in the world.

Character
What does Maribel's comment tell you about Angy's character?

They started making plans to go to the airport with me. They were all talking at once, as usual. "We're going to be there at the airport singing our song for you," they said. It was a song we'd composed describing how we'd gotten together and who we were. The title was "El Combo, No Una Pandilla" (The Combo, Not a Gang).

I explained that seeing them in the airport would make it even worse. Just the idea of not seeing them again was enough to make me cry harder. I'd never graduate with them, go to the prom or on the senior trip.

Make Inferences
Why would it be even harder for Angy to leave if she saw her friends in the airport?

An **Unspoken** Goodbye

My last day of school, in the middle of 7th grade, another friend from school, Sandra, started writing on my white school shirt. She drew a funny girl that looked exactly like her and wrote, "Don't forget about me, girl, and what we went through. You know you're crazy but I love you anyway."

All of a sudden everyone at school was writing on me. They didn't even ask — it was like, grab a pen and write on Angy. Some people I didn't even know were saying good luck and were happy for me.

---

unspoken   not said out loud

74

I walked through the school wearing that written-on shirt, and I never opened my mouth to say goodbye. I tried hard not to cry, so that they'd remember me as they'd always known me — with a big, happy smile.

Painful Regret, Precious Memories

For a while after I moved here, I spoke to Maribel on the phone a lot, but then she moved and I lost touch with her. The last she told me was that "el combito" broke apart.

I painfully regret not saying goodbye, but I knew if I saw them the day I left, I wouldn't be able to get on the plane, and I'd be living miserably there now.

So instead I left quietly, with only the memory of my friends to help me as I struggled to learn to be myself once again, this time in an American world.

Draw Conclusions
Angy says that if she had seen her friends, she wouldn't have been able to get on the plane and would be living miserably in Colombia. Why do you think Angy would have been miserable if she hadn't left?

What Makes a Good Friend?
Why was "el combito" so special to Angy? What qualities did her friends have that made them good friends? Which of these qualities would you look for in a friend? Do you look for friends who are similar to you, or different?

Friendships, like life, are always in a state of change. Do you have the same friends now as you had last year? Sometimes friends relate well to one another; sometimes it seems like they never discuss the real issues. Here, two boys share their very different thoughts on friendship.

Most Guys Need Someone

by Graham, 17, from a suburb in the West

Most guys find it hard to talk about their feelings. I have a big group of friends and we're all pretty comfortable with one another, we all like each other. But we never talk about our feelings unless something is really up.

Most guys need someone to talk to about personal stuff, and they don't have anyone to talk to. Perhaps it's because their dads raised them not to need anyone else's help, and because of that they don't realize they need help even if they do. Many guys don't ask for help: they **repress** their anger and repress their feelings so much they can end up losing it and acting out. Some guys get in lots of fights. It's like when a guy's girlfriend breaks up with him and he's really upset. If he can't talk to anyone, it's likely he'll act out and do something like get in a fight with the ex-girlfriend's new boyfriend.

English Coach
One meaning of *acting out* is "performing a part in a play." Another is "behaving badly." Which meaning of *acting out* is used here?

Just last week one of my friends came to me and was so upset about something that he started crying. He has really liked this girl since June and he thought he was in love with her. She showed some interest and they dated for a while, but now they've stopped dating and he's really upset. She's been toying with him. And now they've broken up, she feels she can't act the same way with him that she does with her other guy friends. For instance, she won't hug him anymore, in case it's **misinterpreted,** but she hugs her casual male friends. That makes it even tougher for him. He's very upset. I just tried to be a good listener.

Draw Conclusions
What information in the paragraph supports the girl's conclusion that a hug might be misinterpreted? Hint: Reread the beginning of the paragraph.

repress to hold in
misinterpreted misunderstood

Guys need to be able to say, "I've got a problem. I can't handle this myself. I need to get it off my chest." And I honestly think that there would be less fighting, less jealousy, and less anger if guys had somebody to talk to about the problems that weigh on their minds.

I would say that about 80 percent of boys go into grade school with high **self-esteem,** and 20 percent go into middle school with high self-esteem. And after high school, only one to 5 percent of high school boys have high self-esteem. And I think the time between sixth grade and senior year is a really hard time to be a guy. Seventh and eighth grades are among the worst. Everyone **harasses** everybody. I got pushed around by the older kids, teased about being small and immature. One of my friends is really skinny and in those years all his jock friends used to tease him.

What Do You Know?
Think about what you know about seventh- and eighth-grade students. Why might these years be especially hard for boys and girls? How did you feel about yourself in the sixth and seventh grades?

---

self-esteem the way a person feels about himself or herself
harasses teases, bothers, or bullies again and again

78

In seventh and eighth grades, people love to pick on you about your physical appearance, your **financial** status, your age, your race, and **sexuality.**

I think a lot of the problems guys have go back to prehistory, the caveman days. The men always went off on hunting trips together, and were in charge of feeding and caring for the family. The men always had to be on guard to protect women and children and they could not open up and bond like the women. The result of all this history is that if a man tries to open up and bond with anyone, it seems like he's acting in a feminine way. And society **disapproves** of that.

We would live in a better society if guys could share their feelings more easily. But guys still hear mixed messages from our society. On the one hand they hear that it's OK now to talk about their feelings, but on the other hand they still hear that they have to be tough and that only girls get **emotional.**

Think About It
During prehistoric times, men hunted for food and women gathered berries and plants. Hunting calls for silence. Gathering allows conversation. What other prehistoric activities might have encouraged men to be silent but allowed women to talk?

financial having to do with money
sexuality feelings and activities related to the attraction between people
disapproves does not support
emotional showing one's feelings

What's the Author's Purpose?

What was the author's purpose in writing this selection? Was he trying to persuade, inform, describe, or entertain? Hint: Remember that an author can have more than one purpose.

My friend who talked to me and cried about his girlfriend was on the football team. His teammates would laugh at him if he tried to talk to them about that sort of stuff. But the fact is that most of them have had similar experiences. And, most of them know how hard it is to feel emotional pain and not talk about it. Some of my friends are like me, and believe guys should talk about their pain and that sharing doesn't make anyone less of a man. But we get mixed messages on this from our parents, our friends, and from society in general.

Our Friendship Is Years Deep

by Rasual, 16, from a city in the East

I met Shareef in elementary school, and we hit it off right away. We could make each other laugh. I like to tell stories, and Shareef was always a good listener. I got to be a better listener from him, and he learned how to relate stories from me.

When Shareef was eleven he developed a problem with his spine called **scoliosis.** He wasn't confined to a wheelchair, but he had to wear a back brace. After that he couldn't run or **vault** fences like he used to. Another thing we used to do before he had his back problem was ride our bikes around and compose **hilarious** rap lyrics.

scoliosis a side-to-side curve of the spine
vault to leap or jump over
hilarious extremely funny

More Information
If scoliosis is detected early, when one is between the ages of 10 and 15, back braces and special exercises can help keep the spine from curving more during growth. People with severe cases may need surgery to straighten their spines.

We came up with some pretty **outrageous** lines, and that sometimes managed to disturb the real serious rappers in the neighborhood. Shareef can't get around too well anymore, and generally he used to be a lot more mobile. Now that I look back at us growing up, it seems that every year his back got a little worse, and there was more he couldn't do.

This summer I joined an **intramural** soccer league. We go around the city and play in different neighborhoods. Shareef and I don't see each other as much as we used to. I know it bothered him at first that I stopped coming around. I thought he might get an attitude about that, but he never did.

English Coach
Here, *attitude* means "a behavior taken for effect." How might Shareef act if he got an attitude about Rasual not coming around?

---

outrageous beyond what is right or proper; shocking
intramural carried on within a school, city, or other area

82

I really respect him for that. For me, though, it was never about whether I wanted to hang out with Shareef or play soccer. It just worked out that way.

When I see Shareef I entertain him with stories about the games and the crazy stuff that goes on, like how sometimes the other team tries to act all tough against us. He tells me about what he's been doing. He's got a girlfriend and they're creating a graphic novel together. Shareef's a computer geek and he's a pro at software design.

Shareef and I have have had our good times, and we've had a lot of laughs and adventures. Who knows what will happen with our friendship? We might grow completely apart or we might not. But that's not getting in the way now. You know, our friendship is years deep. We're just letting it be.

Make Inferences
Do you think Rasual's and Shareef's friendship would have changed if Shareef hadn't gotten scoliosis? Why do you think that?

What Makes a Good Friend?

Is Rasual a good friend to Shareef? Would Graham make a better friend than Rasual? Why or why not? What qualities do most boys look for in a friend? Is it true that boys are less likely than girls to talk about their feelings and problems? Do you agree that society makes it hard for boys to build close friendships? If so, how?

Sailing Away

by Michael Cart

Toby has taken a toy boat to the lake where his best friend, Natty, died in a boating accident. As Toby wades into the water with the boat, he recalls his friendship with Natty. This excerpt begins with a flashback to the past as Toby shares his memories.

More Information

Natty's mother was dead and his father traveled a lot. This helps explain why Toby's parents put up with the friendship and felt sorry for Natty.

Compare and Contrast

Think about the way the author describes Natty and Toby. What do the comparisons tell you about the two boys?

Toby's folks were not so **enthusiastic** about the friendship, but they **tolerated** it because they felt sorry for Natty — well, Toby's mom did, anyway. As for his dad, Toby more than once overheard him grumbling to his wife about things like, "What's wrong with Toby? He lets that kid lead him around by the nose."

Do I? Toby wondered. It had never occurred to him to question the relationship. The sun came up in the east. Natty was the leader. The sun went down in the west. Toby was the follower. It was the natural order of things, as simple and ordinary as breathing.

---

enthusiastic showing great interest or excitement
tolerated put up with

Without Natty, Toby would be only half a person — and the dull half at that, the half that sleepwalked through life. It was Natty who provided the other wide-awake, **vibrant** half, which made Toby feel alive and complete in a way he didn't when he was alone.

At ten, Natty had been a risk taker, a universe disturber. Impatient with rules and order, he insisted on talking to Toby in class, even after their teacher had repeatedly cautioned them to be quiet.

"Stop it," Toby would hiss. "You'll get us in trouble."

"What are you afraid of?" Natty would hiss back.

"I'm not afraid," Toby would insist, shooting an uneasy glance at their teacher. But, of course, he was. And he was secretly glad when Miss Beatty finally separated them, making Natty move to a seat on the other side of the classroom.

---

vibrant full of life and energy

English Coach
Shooting an uneasy glance means "giving an uncomfortable look or expression." Toby gave this look because he wanted to answer Natty, but he was afraid the teacher would catch them talking again.

Think About It
Natty skipped school after his seat was moved. Whom was he acting against — Toby or his teacher? If you are unsure, reread the previous paragraph and this one.

English Coach
A *carnival* is a traveling amusement park with games and rides. The *midway* is the main "road" through the carnival. Have you ever walked down the midway at a carnival? What was it like?

Natty's idea of **retaliation** for that was to skip school the next day and go to the lake. Toby refused to go along for once and, as a result, was miserable the whole day, afraid Natty would be mad and also worried that his friend would get into serious trouble without him. But he didn't. Natty never did. Maybe it was because his father was rich; maybe it was because he was so good-looking that people wanted him to like them. Maybe it was because he never stopped to think about the **consequences** of his actions and so, magically, there weren't any. Whatever the reason, trouble didn't stick to him; it bounced off and stuck to Toby instead.

The first time Toby ever consciously questioned this arrangement was when they were twelve. He and Natty had gone to a carnival and Natty, bored with strolling up and down the midway and eating cotton candy, decided they should ride something called the Bullet.

"Are you crazy?" Toby demanded. Natty knew how much he hated thrill rides.

---

retaliation the act of replying to someone in an unfriendly way
consequences things that happen because of an action or actions

"There's nothing to be afraid of," Natty reassured him. "The ride only lasts a couple of minutes and I'll be in the car with you. Don't be such a big baby. I won't let anything happen to you. Trust me."

As always, Toby gave in.

Natty had been right about one thing: the ride lasted only a couple of minutes, but for Toby it seemed more like an hour in a torture chamber. The tiny bullet-shaped car hurtled through space at nightmare speed, spinning around and around as it **catapulted** to the top of an impossibly high arc and then rocketed back to Earth like a runaway elevator. It grazed the ground before it soared back into the sky, not once but repeatedly. Toby couldn't help himself; he screamed in terror, just as Natty leaned closer to shout, "Having fun yet?"

---

catapulted hurled or threw itself with force and speed

Visualize It
What words and phrases does the author use to help you picture the ride and its speed?

"I hate you," Toby shouted back into Natty's grinning, superior face. And for a second he did, with all his heart. It was the first time he had ever been truly, **viscerally** angry at his friend; and for two days after that, he didn't speak to Natty, freezing him out with an icy silence.

Until Natty apologized. "C'mon," he said, almost pleadingly, "don't be mad at me. I'm sorry. You're like my brother. I need you."

It was the first time he had ever admitted to needing anything. And suddenly he looked so truly **vulnerable,** so **forlorn,** that Toby's iceberg of anger melted away and life gradually returned to normal.

Or as normal as life ever was with Natty.

Toby sighed. The lake didn't seem so cold now, or maybe he was just numb. The wind was still blowing, though, catching the sail of the toy boat and threatening to rip it from his grasp.

More Information

This paragraph returns to the present with Toby at the lake. When the wind catches the sail of the toy boat, it triggers another flashback, or memory, that begins in the next paragraph.

---

viscerally in a way that shows great emotion
vulnerable open to harm or attack, unprotected
forlorn deserted, sad and lonely

The only time Toby had ever been allowed to be captain, a similar wind had actually wrestled the boat from his grasp, and, lunging for it, he caused it to **capsize.**

"Uh-oh," Natty said **ominously.** "You know what that means."

"What?" Toby asked uncertainly.

"It means the captain has to go down with the ship." Natty jumped on him and pulled him down, holding him under water until Toby thought his lungs would burst.

"What are you trying to do," Toby gasped when he finally fought his way to the surface, "kill me?"

---

capsize turn upside-down in the water
ominously in a way that suggests trouble or danger

Character
What does this sentence about Toby tell you about Natty's character? Hint: Think about how often Toby gets to be captain of the boat.

Make Inferences

How do you think Toby felt when Natty gave him a hug? Do you think the hug was enough of an apology from Natty?

Natty just laughed. "Nah," he said. "If I did that, who would I have to **persecute?**" And he gave Toby an awkward, one-armed hug. "C'mon," he said, recovering the boat with an effortless sweep of his other arm, "let's go in and have lunch."

He turned toward shore, and after a minute Toby — his defenses **disarmed** by Natty's unusually clumsy show of affection — shrugged and followed.

---

persecute to annoy or bother
disarmed won over

But he hadn't forgotten the episode. It had become one of a growing number of incidents that he remembered and puzzled over **obsessively** on the rare occasions when he was alone. But it was no use. Natty remained a stubborn mystery. And maybe, after all, that was the secret of his attraction for Toby.

Or maybe — just maybe — the attraction was the same kind of fatal fascination that **immobilizes** a mouse, frozen in its tracks by the **hypnotic** gaze of a hungry snake.

---

obsessively in a way that occupies the mind
immobilizes freezes or keeps from moving
hypnotic holding the attention

Draw Conclusions
What conclusions can you draw about Toby and Natty's friendship based on this comparison?

What Makes a Good Friend?
Who do you think was the better friend — Toby or Natty? Why? Why did Toby continue his friendship with Natty? Think about your closest friend. Is your relationship equal? Or is one of you the leader and the other the follower? Can two people truly be good friends if their friendship is unequal? Why or why not?

In school, it's easy to get caught up in the latest trends. Sometimes it seems like having the coolest new clothes and gear is the only way to fit in. But is it possible to go too far? When two girls find themselves trapped in tough social situations, they each learn their boundaries.

THEY ARE MY FRIENDS

by Margaret Atwood

Character
Authors sometimes let you know what someone is like by describing how others behave toward him or her. Ask yourself what the author wants you to know about the narrator from others' behavior.

Grace is waiting there and Carol, and especially Cordelia. Once I'm outside the house there is no getting away from them. They are on the school bus, where Cordelia stands close beside me and whispers into my ear: "Stand up straight! People are looking!" Carol is in my classroom, and it's her job to report to Cordelia what I do and say all day. They're there at recess, and in the cellar at lunchtime.

They comment on the kind of lunch I have, how I hold my sandwich, how I chew. On the way home from school I have to walk in front of them, or behind. In front is worse because they talk about how I'm walking, how I look from behind. "Don't hunch over," says Cordelia. "Don't move your arms like that."

They don't say any of the things they say to me in front of others, even other children: whatever is going on is going on in secret, among the four of us only. Secrecy is important, I know that: to **violate** it would be the greatest, the **irreparable** sin. If I tell I will be cast out forever.

---

violate break
irreparable unable to be fixed

Draw Conclusions
The narrator worries about being cast out forever. What does this tell you about her relationship with the other three girls?

MIX IT UP:
The Trouble With Fitting In

by Liia Rudolph, age 16

I have a history of changing myself to fit in with the cool crowd.

Starting in fifth grade, I completely changed myself to be a part of the "fabulous five" **clique.** They were a group of 6th-grade girls who wore jeans and tight T-shirts and played truth or dare with boys in the woods.

My main focus in life that year was to become one of them. When the leader of the group, with her brown straight hair, big eyes, and beautiful complexion, told me all I had to do was change my wardrobe, I jumped at the opportunity. On a three-hour trip to the mall, I bought jeans, fitted pants, and T-shirts with sayings like "Princess," "Angel," and "Goddess," to replace the cotton dresses I'd been wearing my whole life.

More Information
"Truth or Dare" is a game in which you must truthfully answer a question or accept a dare, or an unusual challenge.

clique a small group of people who stick together

94

With no regrets, I **sauntered** into school having completely rid myself of the old loser me and ready to welcome the new cool me.

The girls added me to their numbers, making the fabulous five a fabulous six.

When one of them made a comment about my hair lacking shape, I cut it in angles and layers. Anything they wanted, I would get for them. Everything they said, I would do.

From an outsider's view, it might look like I was being used. I guess I was. But I also benefited from the experience in ways that overpowered the social abuse.

After elementary school ended, my clique separated as we all attended different middle schools. I was forced to start over.

Make Inferences
The narrator knows she was being used, or taken advantage of, but says that she gained things in other ways. Based on your experiences, what are the advantages (if any) to belonging to the "cool" crowd?

Although I had been considered cool at my former private and sheltered school, it turned out I knew nothing about popularity and style in the real world of public school.

I was teased miserably. Random girls would ask me why my hair was so greasy. My so-called best friend asked me why I didn't wear makeup to **conceal** my acne.

---

sauntered   strolled or walked at a relaxed pace
conceal   hide from view

There still was only one thing I wanted — to be accepted and popular. So I began my second major change.

'Desperate measures'

I met a popular girl who "let" me be her friend and helped me **transform.** We worked out together. She did my makeup until I was a pro at it myself. And she talked me through fashion and let me wear her clothes.

I soon discovered middle school students are much more ruthless than elementary school kids. My changes weren't occurring quickly enough and I wasn't accepted as I knew I should be.

This called for desperate measures.

Learning all of my tactics from health class, I began monitoring my diet. As the weight dropped, people were drawn to me. I hadn't been overweight before, but now I looked like the starving models all the popular girls **strived** to be.

Now that I had acquired a beautiful and popular best friend, stylish clothing, and a flawless **physique,** I was all set.

---

transform change in form or appearance
strived tried hard
physique the human body and its appearance

Think About It
Note the headings in this selection. How can these headings help you preview important ideas?

English Coach
Ruthless means "showing no pity, cruel." In what ways can middle school students be ruthless?

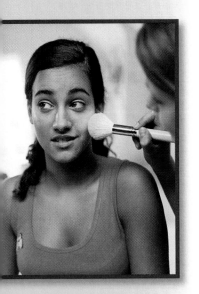

But along with these new aspects of my life, I lost my values. I had always been a good girl, following almost every rule. Within a year, I had broken all of the promises I had made to myself. Too swept up in the energy of the crowd and the **encouragement** of my new best friend, I never even thought about what I was doing.

'A lesson to learn'

My connection to popularity was lost a year later after the friendship with my best friend and partner-in-crime broke up, leaving me an overly made up, skinny, lonely, lost girl.

I spent the next few months miserable. Having lost the energy to make myself look "good," I wore sweatpants and T-shirts (without "Princess" slogans) to school. My eye makeup disappeared and my hair went back to its natural wavy state.

I had come to the conclusion that no one would want to talk to me now that I wasn't cool, but I couldn't have been more wrong.

People I had treated horribly made an effort to befriend me. Instead of partying and watching my friends drink and make out with boys, I went out and watched movies and ate personal pizzas.

encouragement the act of giving confidence or hope

Visualize It
As you read the next two paragraphs, try to picture the narrator as she looked when she was a part of the "in" crowd and how she looked afterwards. What do you see as the greatest change?

What's the Author's Purpose?
Why did the narrator write this selection — to inform, describe, persuade, or entertain? Perhaps she had more than one purpose. Who was her intended audience?

The people I had gossiped about and badmouthed were the ones to accept me as I really was. It was quite a lesson to learn.

When I finally broke down and was able to show the real me, true friends came to me. I learned forgiveness from them.

Compare and Contrast
How are the relationships in this selection like the ones in "They Are My Friends"? How are they different?

Friendship and life are not about who's wearing what or who is hooking up with whom or where the big party is. They are about loving people for their true selves and learning from their **quirks** and differences.

Finally, I am able to express myself and be happy with who I am instead of always trying to fake it.

---

quirks odd habits or behaviors

What Makes a Good Friend?

Does belonging to the "in crowd" mean that you will have good friends? Why or why not? How far would you go to fit in? What would you do to make new friends? What would you do to hold on to the ones you have? Is it possible to make a true friend if you are not true to yourself?

Unit 4

What Makes Me Healthy?

What does it mean to be healthy? Health means different things to different people. We feel our best when our bodies, minds, and emotions are all in good health.

There are many roads to health. Some challenge the body; others exercise the mind. A few do both and help to shape people's lives in many ways.

You make many choices every day that can add up to good health. How do you know which choices are right for you? Sometimes health begins with trying new things.

Yoga *for* Teens

by Bess Gallanis

Yoga is an ancient system of mental and physical exercise that was developed in what is now India. Followers use yoga to improve their health and to achieve peace of mind. Recently, teens have taken up yoga in huge numbers. Why are so many teens trying yoga? Read on to find out.

Behind the purple door of a storefront building set back from a tree-lined street in Highland Park, Illinois, 16-year-old Ava Friedman removes her shoes and softly pads into Heart Center Yoga. Seeing her friends already seated in half lotus, she quietly **unfurls** a purple yoga mat, arranges blue foam blocks and a canvas strap within reach, then folds a thick cotton blanket into thirds. She takes her own seat in half lotus and begins to focus on her breathing.

---

unfurls unrolls or unfolds

English Coach
Half lotus is a yoga position in which the person sits with the left leg placed up onto the right thigh and the right leg tucked under. Can you sit in a half lotus?

A few minutes later Ava and her fellow teenage yoginis are performing sun **salutations** to the music of the Dixie Chicks.

"You can really work up a sweat and build muscles in yoga," says Ava later, a serious yogini who **practices** once or twice a week in a studio. "But it's also a total break from my day. When I'm practicing yoga I am not thinking about anything else."

Demand for yoga classes from teenagers is **accelerating** as more and more young people like Ava view yoga as the on-ramp to a healthier lifestyle. Contemporary teenagers are the most health-conscious generation ever. It may seem **contradictory,** given the problem of obesity and **deteriorating** fitness of our nation's kids. Nonetheless, "work out" is the first thing teenage girls say they choose to do in their spare time. And yoga is the fastest growing fitness activity.

English Coach
A *yogini* is "a female who practices yoga." Males who practice yoga are called *yogi* or *yogin*. If you practiced yoga, what would you be called?

What Do You Know?
Do you know anyone who practices yoga? Do you practice yoga? What do you know about it?

salutations greetings
practices does over and over to gain skill
accelerating becoming greater, increasing
contradictory expressing the opposite
deteriorating becoming worse

Staying healthy means a lot more to kids today than avoiding a cold. Boys and girls both are concerned about eating well, getting more exercise, and managing stress. But teenagers also say they are looking for something to help them make sense of a **chaotic** world. They find yoga's inner focus a spiritual experience. They also are looking for tools to help them manage stress.

Teenagers are tribal and want to practice yoga with their peers, to their own music and in their own space.

During most of her life, Ava has watched her mom, Sari Gluckin, practice yoga. Yet, when given the opportunity, Ava preferred to practice with other teenagers twice a week. Sari asked Heart Center Yoga owner, Ilene Sang, if she would put a teen class on the studio's schedule. Sari and Ava **recruited** six Highland Park High School girls, who met at Heart Center to practice with Susan Star, a local yoga teacher.

---

chaotic completely out of order and confused
recruited convinced to join

"Susan listened to the girls and experimented to see what worked," says Ilene. "She had a pretty stable group of six girls who practiced together. They were very serious, probably because they were a little older. They liked practicing to Dave Matthews Band."

"What these teens really want is permission to rest," says Ilene, **perceptively.**

The sound of a small gong brings five Deerfield High School girls to attention. As they cross their legs and get comfortable on mats, which are organized in a circle so they are facing each other, Ilene explains today's theme is a letting-go practice.

---

perceptively knowingly, with understanding

Draw Conclusions
The yoga teachers set up special classes for teens and experimented to see what worked. What conclusions can you draw from this? Would this work for every type of sport or art form?

103

"Right now, stop thinking," she **intones.** "Just listen to my voice. Don't think. Just be here. Listen. Breathe." A few minutes later, they begin performing sun salutations to "Songs from a Secret Garden" and end their practice with an extended **savasana.** The girls raise themselves to hands and knees, crawl to the center of their circle and take a deep group breath.

Asked what they're taking off the mat and into life, 14-year-old Lily Seglin says, "When I'm mad, I breathe." Learning how to manage powerful emotions like frustration, anger, and confusion is one of the many reasons teenagers seek out yoga.

In Vernon Hills, Total Body Studio owner Silvia Mordini received a phone call from the parent of a football player about creating a yoga class for the football team. "The demand for yoga came directly from the guys," says Silvia. "They had done their homework about yoga and learned how professional athletes practice yoga to prevent injuries."

Make Inferences
Based on the information in this paragraph and your own experiences, how would you describe the lives of teenagers? Why would teenagers need something like yoga?

---

intones says in a singing tone; chants
savasana a yoga position that allows the body to relax by lying on the back in a quiet place with the arms beside the body, palms up

Over the summer, nine 17-year-old seniors who play on the school's varsity football team, the Cougars, practiced yoga once a week at Total Body.

"I love the stretch and relaxation I get from practicing yoga," says 17-year-old **defensive** linebacker Zax Foster, who practices yoga to improve his athletic performance. "Silvia really understands us," he says.

At Walter Payton High School, Dina Pingeton's fitness class is being guided through a stress-releasing exercise. Dina asks them to prepare to release stress from their bodies by creating a stress ball. They are to **visualize** all their stress beginning to take shape in a big ball. When they are ready, students are asked to imagine throwing the stress ball into a fire or the ocean. They are to imagine it **receding** into the horizon until the ball is no longer visible.

Visualize It
Picture in your mind the stress-releasing exercise described here. Where will you throw your stress ball?

---

defensive belonging to the team that tries to keep the other team from scoring
visualize form a picture in the mind
receding going away, moving back

"The kids are incredibly imaginative during the stress ball exercise; they go all sorts of places to throw that ball away," she says. "The classes are **coed,** so you get some **self-consciousness.** The boys won't take off their socks. But all in all, I get a lot of positive feedback from the kids, their parents, and other teachers at school."

One of the more **innovative** teen yoga classes in the area is taught by Brian Tennison, an intense and popular history teacher at Whitney Young High School.

"Yoga is a real draw to the class," says 17-year-old Margaret Sharp. "It's very cool and you do feel different after practicing yoga. But it's also very cool to take the class. It's very unique to take Asian studies in high school."

One sunny morning early in the school year, the Whitney Young seniors move their desks to the **perimeter** of the room, shoving some into the hall, to make way for a yoga studio.

Ask Questions
To make sure you understand what you're reading, pause once in a while to ask yourself questions such as: *What is this paragraph about? Who is involved? Why? When? Where? How?*

---

coed having both male and female members
self-consciousness being so aware of how you look to others that you are embarrassed
innovative introducing new methods
perimeter the outside walls of a room

"Find some space," Brian calls out to the students. "Stand in the middle of your space. Claim it." Students claim their space on an **array** of purple yoga mats and beach towels.

"Take your seat," he calls out. Obediently, 25 high school seniors sit down and cross their legs. Breathing exercises begin and within a few minutes the entire room sounds like a seashell. Today, the students are practicing sun salutations, which Brian explains is a morning practice to prepare one's body for the day ahead.

"Feet down, energy down, open your fingers wide," he intones. "Open up those energy channels."

"The conditions are a little rough, but I try hard to give them a physical class," Brian says later.

"I tell my students they can't fail, there is no failure in yoga."

---

array orderly arrangement

What's the Author's Purpose?
Why do you think the author wrote this selection? Hint: Was the author trying to entertain, persuade, describe, or inform?

What Makes Me Healthy?

Why are so many teens choosing yoga as a form of exercise? How are teens' lives changed by doing yoga? Would you like to give yoga a try? Why or why not? What do you like to do to keep your body and mind healthy?

Doctor Robot Will See You Now

What would you do if at your next doctor's appointment a robot showed up instead of your doctor? Doctors and hospitals have begun using special robots to check in with their patients and to perform operations. In the health care field, some things that were science fiction are now science fact.

If you are a fan of science fiction, you've probably read stories about robots. Often these fictional robots can think and move around all by themselves. Some even look just like humans. In reality, robots still depend upon humans to tell them what to do. But there has been an upgrade in robots' abilities, especially in the health care sciences. And some robots can do many things as well as — or even better than — a human can.

Registered Nurse Emmy Degui talks with a robot who is controlled by Dr. Garth Ballantyne (on screen) at the Hackensack University Medical Center.

Doctors in hospitals are using robots to help them perform both simple and difficult tasks that doctors usually do. One of the most popular of these robots roams hospital halls in the form of a doctor robot, a five-and-a-half-foot-tall, 200-pound **android.**

This doctor robot is actually known as a **mobile teleconferencing** robot, and human doctors use it to make patient rounds by remote control when they can't visit patients in person. The robot has a flat-screen monitor for a head and video cameras that perform as its eyes and ears. The doctor's face appears on the robot's monitor, which gives the effect of the doctor being present wherever the robot goes. A doctor operates the robot, using a joystick, from another building or sometimes even another country, by way of the Internet and wireless links.

English Coach
Round usually describes something with a circular shape. Here, *rounds* refers to routes around the hospital that doctors take to visit patients. What other professionals make rounds on their jobs?

android a machine made in the shape of a human
mobile easily moved from one place to another
teleconferencing communicating among people in different locations through special equipment

Using a laptop computer to link to the screen on the robot's head, the doctor communicates with the patient through a live video feed. The doctor can have a conversation with the patient, examine stitches, and even brag about his or her golf game — without ever leaving the office!

The robot doctor may look like just a rolling, wireless laptop perched upon a metal **cylinder,** but it does a pretty good job of holding a conversation. The doctor can operate the robot's monitor head from his or her computer so that the robot's "face" turns toward the person who is speaking. This gives the conversation a more natural feeling, especially when there are more than two people involved.

Find the Details
The main idea of this paragraph is that robots make it easier for doctors to do their jobs. How do robots help doctors do their jobs more efficiently?

The purpose of using robots in this way isn't to replace human doctors. It is simply to make it easy for a doctor to be in two places at the same time. In addition, it allows the patient to have more and better **access** to his or her doctor. Doctors also can use the robots to help them decide whether they need to deal with situations in person.

---

cylinder a solid figure with two round ends, like a can
access the ability to approach or meet with someone

For example, a patient in the hospital may wake up at two o'clock in the morning with a pain or other problem. The doctor can call the robot doctor from home and quickly **dispatch** it to the patient's bedside to find out the how serious the problem is.

Many hospitals lack the funds to keep certain **specialists** as full-time staff. But with robot doctors, patients may one day **consult** with specialists from remote locations wherever and whenever these experts are needed. A kidney specialist in Delhi, India, might teleconference with a patient-care team in Kalamazoo, Michigan. This teleconferencing will no doubt help to save time and lives.

For now, though, robot doctors are used mostly to check on patients in between actual visits from a living, breathing doctor. Some people might think patients would feel a little strange when it comes to talking to a machine about their health. But studies have shown that most patients don't mind it. Some even enjoy it. More than half of the patients who were asked said they'd rather be visited by their own doctor through a robot's live video hookup than be visited by an unknown doctor.

Make Inferences
How would teleconferencing save time and lives? Use the situation described in the second-to-last sentence of this paragraph as an example.

dispatch to send off
specialists doctors who are experts in certain medical areas
consult to exchange information

This robot hand moves from the wrist the same way that a human hand does.

Graphic Sources
Headings are titles for sections of text. You can use headings to help you predict what you will read next. What do you think you will read about in this section?

Robots in the Operating Room

Robot technology has also moved into the operating room. In many hospitals, **surgical** robots are actually used to operate on patients. These robots do not act like or look like the robots who visit patients on daily rounds. Surgical robots mainly consist of multiple arms, with joints that act like elbows, wrists, and hands — kind of like a mechanical octopus. These robots are able to perform many simple surgical tasks. Just like the rolling robot doctors, these machines act only under a doctor's commands. The robot **surgeon** receives its instructions from a human surgeon who, in most cases, is seated several feet away at a viewing station.

---

surgical related to an operation to repair the body
surgeon a doctor who operates to repair a patient's body

He or she controls the **surgery** by looking at a 3-D visual image of the operation taking place across the room. As the doctor's fingers grasp the master controls at the station, the computer arms smoothly translate the surgeon's hand, wrist, and finger movements into accurate, real-time movements.

Robots are able to perform some surgical functions even better than humans can. They are able to move and position surgical instruments with 100 percent accuracy. Unlike human doctors, robots never get tired. And even the most skilled human surgeon's hands aren't as steady as the hands of a robot. The robot's movements are controlled by the surgeon, but the computer adjusts for any errors. That means that even if the surgeon's hand shakes when moving the controls, the robot's hand will remain steady.

Draw Conclusions
What conclusion can you draw from the fact that robots can position instruments with 100 percent accuracy, they never get tired, and their "hands" never shake?

surgery an operation to repair the body

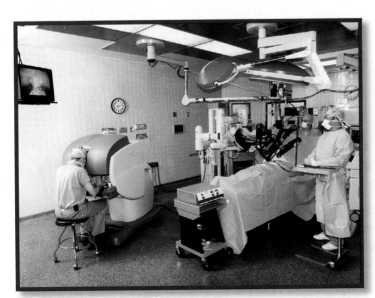

A surgeon can operate on a patient, using robot controls and a 3-D viewing screen, while sitting several feet away.

As time goes on, robots will be able to handle more and more complex surgical procedures. That will mean fewer people will be needed in the operating room. And that could lead to lower costs and less risk of infection for patients.

Robots in Our Future

Many people feel that robot technology is going to make as big a difference in this century as computers did in the last one. Robots can be easily programmed to perform the same steps over and over again in exactly the same way. For example, they are already used on factory assembly lines to speed up production.

Summarize It

After reading, it's a good idea to summarize what you've read to be sure you understood all the important points. Briefly summarize this selection, using the questions *Who? What? Where? When? Why?* and *How?*

This is an artist's drawing of the robot rover "Spirit," one of the twin robots that gathered information on Mars in 2003. The robot was about the size of a riding lawn mower.

In recent years, companies have been building robots to help with chores such as mowing the lawn, cleaning the house, and even planting trees. Robots have been sent to places too dangerous for humans to visit. Special robots have explored deep trenches in the ocean floor, where the extreme underwater pressure could squash a submarine. They have also rolled across the rocky, airless **terrain** of distant planets.

It looks as though robots will be helping humans for a long time to come. People who work in health care are happy with the arrangement. Doctors and robots have what some might call a very healthy relationship.

---

terrain an area of land

What Makes Me Healthy?

Regular visits to the doctor are a good way to stay healthy. How are robots helping doctors meet their patients' needs for health care? Do you think using robots is a good idea? How would you feel about talking to a robot about your health or letting a robot operate on you? Can you think of any other ways in which technology has already changed your life?

Getting a Kick Out of Martial Arts

by Mariana Relos

Karate, kung fu, and judo are only a few of the Asian martial arts that are now practiced around the world. Although they were developed thousands of years ago, these ancient arts are very popular today. Through graceful fighting, millions of teens have found a new sense of strength.

Draw Conclusions
How good is Jules at running laps on the track? What information helped you figure that out?

On your mark! Get set! Go! Jules started to sweat just hearing those words. He might be a straight-A student in class, but when it came to running laps on the track, he got D's. Jules wished he could run at least half the number of laps most of his classmates ran. For Jules, the worst part wasn't the fact that he was the slowest, least-fit kid in his class. The worst was that his classmates teased him about it. Fortunately for Jules, he found a solution to his problem during a school carnival day.

A **martial arts** school gave a demonstration. Kids in black uniforms tied with colorful belts kicked, jumped, and yelled with amazing energy. Jules wanted to have that kind of energy. He decided to try martial arts. He talked to his parents about it and convinced them to let him sign up for a trial class.

From Asia . . .

The oldest martial arts are at least 1,400 years old. They began in China, Japan, and Korea. People developed martial arts to defend themselves and their property from thieves. They used just their hands and feet. In Japan, soldiers practiced martial arts to become better fighters. In China, monks usually spent long hours sitting while they **meditated** or wrote. The lack of exercise made their bodies weak. They practiced martial arts to stay fit.

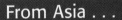

martial arts any of several Asian methods of self-defense
meditated thought quietly and deeply over a period of time

English Coach
Trial often means "a court process to judge whether charges are true or false." Here, *trial* means "a tryout." Jules can attend a trial class to see if he wants to sign up for more martial arts classes. Have you ever gone to a trial class or used a trial product?

What Do You Know?
Chinese actor Jackie Chan is an excellent martial artist. Have you seen any Jackie Chan movies? If so, how would you describe them?

Chinese karate and *kung fu* use mostly hand strikes for attack and defense. Jackie Chan is a famous kung fu master. *Karate* means "free hand."

Judo is one of the oldest Japanese martial arts. It uses grabbing and throwing techniques to defeat an opponent. The president of Russia, Vladimir Putin, regularly practices judo. *Judo* means "gentle way."

Tae kwon do is a Korean martial art. It combines hand techniques and kicking for defense and attack. *Tae kwon do* means "art of kicking and punching." This is the favorite Korean martial art in the United States.

Today, martial arts are very popular all over the world. There are at least 55 recognized martial arts. They all use hand techniques and kicking. In the United States, about 18 million people practiced a martial art in 2003. About 3 million of them were children, and about 6 million were teenagers. A study has shown that children do not practice martial arts only for **self-defense.** Most kids have found out that practicing these ancient arts benefits many other features of their lives.

Good for Body and Mind

Jules could not believe it. After just six months of practicing martial arts for an hour at least three times a week, he could run 10 laps around the school track without stopping. He didn't finish first, but he didn't have to stop to catch his breath either.

Jules's classmates noticed he was doing better in track. They slowly stopped teasing him. This helped him feel more comfortable around his classmates. Jules feels much better about himself now. He plans to continue practicing martial arts for as long as he can. Like Jules, many kids who regularly practice martial arts improve their physical and mental skills. They also have higher **self-esteem.**

---

self-defense guarding or protecting yourself
self-esteem the way a person feels about himself or herself

What's the Main Idea?
The main idea of this paragraph is stated clearly. Which sentence tells what the paragraph is mostly about?

Find the Details
What details support the idea that practicing martial arts helped Jules?

Charles L. Richman is a professor of psychology and director of the martial arts program at Wake Forest University in North Carolina. He says that "a martial arts program will help almost anyone develop quicker reaction time, better **coordination,** and greater concentration at any age." Studies have shown that kids who practice martial arts usually perform better in school. They normally have better **self-discipline.**

Students of a Korean martial art called *Kuk Sool Won* have found that it has helped them in many ways. "Since I joined Kuk Sool Won six years ago, I've gotten stronger, and I have more endurance," says Sumit, 13. "I was very shy, but now I am more **outgoing** and have made new friends. I feel much better about myself."

---

coordination a smooth working together of the parts of the body
self-discipline control of your emotions or actions to improve yourself
outgoing easy to meet and talk to; friendly

Other students have discovered that Kuk Sool Won has helped them to control their temper. Elana, 15, believes that martial arts have taught her a way to get along better with people. Emerald, 16, says, "By practicing martial arts, I got skills I did not have before. I am stronger and quicker."

Martial Arts and More

Martial arts can help you perform better in other sports. Three-time world figure skating champion Elvis Stojko practices kung fu. It improves his balance, **flexibility,** and concentration. This has made him a better figure skater. He believes that martial arts can help many people improve in any sport, training, or practice.

---

flexibility ability to bend or be bent easily

Summarize It
Briefly summarize the many ways that martial arts help kids. Remember to include only the most important details in your summary.

Narrative or Informational?
Is this selection narrative or informational? Hint: Think about whether it tells a story or gives facts about a topic.

The Japanese baseball player Sadaharu Oh believes that *aikido* has improved his game. "Without aikido, I would not learn to stand on one foot," he says.

Seth is 13 and loves to play soccer. But he had a hard time keeping up with this high-paced game. "After I started Kuk Sool Won, I began having more energy. I could run longer during soccer games. I played better and had a good time," he says.

Martial Arts for All

Jules noticed that all kinds of kids attend martial arts classes and benefit from them. Overweight kids have a tough time at the beginning. But after a few months, they **literally** "kick the pounds away." They get leaner and lighter and begin to improve their skills.

Kids with special needs — like Amanda, who has **cerebral palsy** — have improved their physical condition. Amanda cannot control her muscles very well. But she has improved. She believes it is because of karate practice. The only thing Amanda could do in gym class before was keep score.

---

literally actually; really
cerebral palsy a disability caused by damage to the brain before, during, or shortly after birth that can affect movement and speech

Now she practices one-hour workouts that test her endurance and strength. "Karate changed my life," she says. "It is my favorite thing to do in the whole world."

Ask Questions
You can check your understanding after reading a selection by asking yourself questions like *Who? What? Where? When? Why?* and *How?* What questions could you ask yourself about this selection?

What Makes Me Healthy?
Martial arts are ancient forms of exercise that have very modern uses. How are people today using martial arts to help themselves both physically and mentally? Which martial art might you like to try? Why? How can being physically healthy help you in other areas of your life?

The Crash Room

by David Rice

In a hospital emergency room (ER), life is always on the line. Doctors and nurses rush to save lives — but they don't always succeed. How do ER doctors stay positive when things don't work out? Here, one young man learns what inspires him to help others.

What Do You Know?
What is the golden rule? How do you think someone working in a hospital could apply it?

The best thing about working at the hospital was that I got to help people. I tried to follow the golden rule. If patients were cold (and you know how cold hospitals are), I would give them a blanket. If they looked real cold or were elderly, they got heated blankets.

It was cool when the doctors in ER asked for me. Since I spoke Spanish, I could translate for them.

I would go into ER and talk to the patients and try to make them more comfortable, because being a patient is no fun, especially if you don't understand a word of what is being said all around you. I imagined it must be like being **abducted** by a UFO.

I was thrilled about **surgery** and the **trauma** rooms. Although I never got a chance to watch any surgeries, I did see much in the crash room, where a ballet of lab and x-ray techs, nurses, and doctors took place whenever a patient came in.

In order to be a patient in the crash room, you had to be a Code Three. There were four types of codes. Code One meant you may not feel well, so you'll just have to sit until we get to you, and in the meantime you'll see people who make your **petty** pain feel silly.

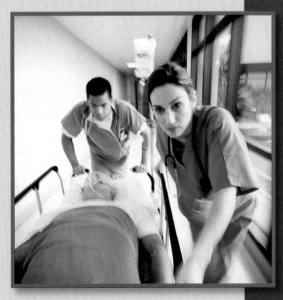

---

abducted kidnapped; carried off against your will
surgery an operation to repair the body
trauma a severe physical injury
petty not important

Compare and Contrast
To what does the author compare being a patient who can't understand English? Is this a good comparison? Why or why not?

Code Two meant that you're probably bleeding and you went ahead of Code One. Code Three was serious, because you are a mess. The crash room was created for folks who may not make it. Code Three was the center of the dance. Code Four meant you were dead. The ambulance drivers would be speeding to Brackenridge with the Code Three patient, and the crash team would be getting ready, but then the drivers would radio in a Code Four and the team would stand down.

But when a Code Three came in, with the patient holding on for dear life, people would be flying in and out of the crash room. Most of the time there would be blood all over the floor, and medical staff left footprints in blood all over ER and down the halls.

Nurses would simply tear away at the packages containing medical equipment and throw the trash on the floor. Everyone had a duty; I.V.'s were started, heart **monitors** put in place, x-rays were taken, doctors specializing in whatever was the main problem would shout out orders, and people moved — not for the doctors, mind you, but for the patient. It was a rush.

---

monitors devices that allow people to be observed constantly

Summarize It
Briefly tell in your own words what the four codes are and what each one means.

English Coach
I.V. is short for *intravenous*, which means "within or into a vein." Doctors and nurses sometimes give medicine, blood, or other fluids to a patient directly into his or her veins.

I saw one person die in the crash room and others who died hours or days later. Many times the patient would go straight to surgery from the crash room and the wheels of the stretcher left blood trails. Sometimes I would help lift the patient, and blood would drench the **latex** gloves that covered my hands. Watching someone else's blood drip down from my fingers to the floor always made me think that somehow it was my blood.

After two years at Brackenridge I began not to like myself. I had become rather **insensitive** to people's pain and suffering. If I saw someone crying about his minor pains, I would say things like, "Oh, quit your whining." It was an attitude I had picked up from others in the department and throughout the hospital.

This insensitivity was affecting my entire personality. At school I was beginning to have difficulty making friends and keeping girlfriends. Girls I liked said I was **callous,** and Roger was considered the sweet brother, while I was the jerk brother.

Character
Authors usually let you know what someone is like by describing him or her. Here the narrator describes himself and tells what others think of him. What phrases in this paragraph and the next one help you understand his character?

---

latex rubber made from the sticky white juice that comes from certain plants, such as rubber trees
insensitive not noticing, or not taking the care to notice, other people's feelings
callous not caring

127

Worse yet, I didn't feel like being a doctor anymore. I didn't see what good all this medicine and medical equipment were doing. Every now and then I would get happy about some patient making a wonderful **recovery,** but usually it was only because their family members were there every day to support them. The elderly seem to die alone many times. The whole place was **depressing** me. I knew that I had to quit this job.

Six years later, I was dating Marie, who was an x-ray tech at Brackenridge when I worked there. Marie worked at yet another hospital. Brackenridge was now just a big hospital off Interstate 35, and when I drove by it, I was glad I wasn't there.

But one Christmas season, after I had married Marie, we found ourselves standing in the Brackenridge ER crash room, next to my brother Roger, who lay dying on a **stretcher.** I was dazed as I stood there. Marie held my hand to give me hope, but we had seen Roger's CAT scan, and he was a mess. He wasn't going anywhere except down to the basement, through the darkness, and into the garden.

---

recovery return to health after sickness or injury
depressing making sad or gloomy
stretcher a strip of canvas supported by long poles and used to carry sick people

English Coach
Tech is short for *technician.* An x-ray technician is someone who is skilled at taking and reading x-rays. What other kinds of techs can you think of?

More Information
A CAT scan is a picture produced by a machine that combines x-rays. Each shows a different cross section of a part of the body.

We knew most of the medical staff, some of whom were even at our wedding, and they all expressed their sorrow. I knew they had done their best because the crash room floor was littered with wrappers and covered in blood. It was a bad auto accident that Roger had been in, leaving him brain dead. This beautiful, brown, athletic twenty-four-year-old now lived only through machines. His soul was ready to fly.

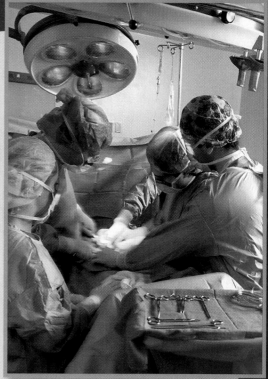

I spoke to him. I told him he was in the crash room. I told him that this was serious stuff, to quit playing around. But Roger never listened to me. He would just walk away with a wave of his hand. But I held his hand tight, wanting him to stay.

His death changed my life. At the wake his friends from the Army and countless of his girlfriends talked about how fast he was. How he ran every day, no matter what the weather. He was training to be the fastest in his army division and was a mere second behind the leader. If he could be the fastest, then I could be a doctor.

Find the Details
What details support the idea that the narrator's life was changed by his brother's death?

Medical school wasn't easy for me, but I studied every day. I imagined I was in a race and that becoming a doctor was crossing the finishing line. When things got hard I pretended Roger was there, urging me on as I did him at his track meets.

I now walk the halls of the hospital with a white lab coat on and **stethoscope** around my neck and a badge that says Dr. Eduardo Cuellar Aguilar. When I work my shift in ER and hear the ambulance drivers say they have a Code Three coming in, I feel the blood rushing into my legs for a race I always want to win.

stethoscope an instrument that doctors use to listen to sounds made by the heart and lungs

Narrative or Informational?
Is this selection narrative or informational? Hint: Remember that narrative texts tell stories and informational texts give facts.

What Makes Me Healthy?
What did the narrator like about working in the hospital at first? What made him change his mind and quit working there? How did his brother's death affect his plans to become a doctor? Would you like to work in a hospital? Why or why not? What do you think inspires people to choose careers in which they help others? In what ways can helping others make you healthy?

What Can Journeys Teach?

Where can a journey take you, and what can you learn there? Some journeys take you to new places. You might experience a new culture in a distant country or learn about nature in a park or a museum close to home. Other journeys take you inside your mind, where you might discover something new about yourself.

People have taken many exciting and important journeys throughout history. In this unit, you will meet some people who took long journeys and others who traveled shorter distances but learned just as much.

An Exchange Student at 17

by Elaine Abonal

Journeys take us outside of our everyday experience. They often open our minds to new ways of thinking about ourselves and others. Elaine Abonal, an exchange student from the Philippines, found that a year in Wisconsin gave her a new view of the world — and a new source of confidence.

More information

The Philippines is a country made up of about 7,000 islands in the southwest Pacific Ocean. Manila, the capital, is the largest city. Filipino (based on Tagalog) and English are the official languages.

What's the Author's Purpose?

Why do you think Elaine wrote about her experience as an exchange student? Hint: Remember that authors usually write to inform, to persuade, to describe, or to entertain.

It feels as if it was just yesterday when I was on my own on a plane — not really knowing what to expect, but excited for what the future held. Now I'm back home with a ton of memories, e-mails to answer, and a lot of stories to share. I don't even know where to start now that I'm writing about my experience of being an exchange student in Appleton, Wisconsin, for a whole school year.

I've wanted to be an exchange student my whole high school life. I read about summer programs in

a **brochure** from IFS, and I thought then that living somewhere else for a while and having friends from another country would be the coolest thing in the world. I researched Wisconsin in books and on the Internet. Compared to what I saw on TV and what I experienced when I traveled to places like Los Angeles, California, with my family, Wisconsin was different. It had more farmland and countryside. Appleton's population was around 70,000. I thought it was a small town compared to our Manila. There was no traffic, they only had one major mall, and everything was in close **proximity.**

brochure a short booklet that contains information
proximity nearness; closeness

More Information
IFS stands for the Philippines' Institute for Foreign Study. IFS offers summer programs for students from 9 to 24 years old and school-year programs for students from 15 to 18.

Make Inferences
What can you infer about winter in the Philippines from Elaine's description of winter in Wisconsin?

I didn't even know what to think of the cold weather. I brought only cotton long-sleeved shirts with me. But when winter came, I needed to get a coat. During the winter, the sun set at 4 p.m. and didn't go up until around 9. There were days when the temperature went below freezing and I wore 6 layers of clothing just to keep myself warm. I had never even blow-dried my hair before. In Appleton, I had to do it every morning after I took a shower because if I didn't, my hair would FREEZE. The thing I liked best about the cold and the snow was being able to ski. I had never skied in my life, so I was excited and proud to learn.

Elaine skis with friends.

Elaine with some members of her host family

I was placed with the greatest **host** family in the whole world. They treated me like their own, and they are like real family in another part of the world. I had a host mom, a host dad, and a brother and sister, named Ben and Katie. I felt super loved. They made sure there was tuna in the pantry (since it was my favorite), and hugged me when I needed to be hugged.

I went to an American co-ed public high school, which was a big **adjustment** coming from an all-girl private Catholic school in the Philippines. The school was new, and it was so **diverse** — I have never met so many kinds of people in just one place. I was scared during the first day of school. I didn't know anyone, and I got lost, since the school was huge.

English Coach
Co-ed is short for *coeducational,* which means "having boys and girls at the same school." Was Elaine's school in the Philippines co-ed? Why or why not?

---

host a person who entertains guests or welcomes strangers into his or her home
adjustment the process of getting used to a change
diverse made up of people from many different backgrounds

Find the Details
What details support the idea that the students at Elaine's high school didn't know very much about the Philippines?

People didn't think I knew how to speak in English because my teachers introduced me by saying, "And here's Elaine — she's a foreign exchange student." But pretty soon I started to get comfortable. It was funny how people were always surprised by how good I was at speaking in English. They said, "Wow, you even speak better English than me." I loved answering people's questions like, "So, what do you do in the winter?" or "Where is the Philippines? Isn't that near South America somewhere?" or "What's it like to have a coconut tree outside your house — do you have coconuts every day?" I was also an **honorary** member of the International Club. One time I was giving a talk about the Philippines for the school's Global Awareness Week, and someone asked me to say something in Filipino. So I said, "Magandang Umaga, ang pangalan ko ay Elaine." People clapped and gave me a standing **ovation** — just for saying my name in Tagalog!

I made a lot of friends and met so many people. I joined a church youth group, volunteered for a group for teens with **cognitive disabilities,** played on an indoor soccer team during winter, and ran on the girl's track team during spring.

---

honorary   chosen out of respect
ovation   a loud burst of applause
cognitive disabilities   problems with the brain that affect learning

Friends took me out to movies, hockey games, restaurants, road trips, rock shows, and concerts. Everyone was warm, open, and never **hesitant** to give hugs. As much as I missed my family and friends at home, I never really got homesick because I had friends who made sure I was okay.

One of the things I had to get used to and eventually enjoyed was how people picked up on my difference. Girls would always tell me how lucky I was to have a "year-round tan" and ask if I went to tanning salons! I haven't even heard of tanning salons before I got there! Some boys would ask me how I got my hair to be "so black."

---

hesitant not sure or not willing

English Coach
Exotic means "excitingly different or unusual." People or things from a foreign country often seem exotic. What seems exotic to you?

More Information
Adobo is a Philippine dish of meat or fish soaked in a sauce and seasoned with garlic, soy sauce, vinegar, and spices.

This opened my eyes to more similarities and differences between the Filipino and American cultures. It was one of the times I was so proud of being Filipina. I was different, exotic, and new.

Every month, I met with other exchange students in our area. I made friends with people from Germany, Brazil, the Netherlands, England, Hungary, etc. It was fun when we were together because we saw how language, skin color, or height didn't matter. We were all the same. We **bonded** right away because we were all going through the same thing as exchange students, and we talked about the differences between our homes, schools, and our countries. I learned so many things about other cultures, and even got to share my own. I remember cooking the *adobo* for a Christmas party. I was stressed about it but everyone loved it!

bonded became friends

The Filipino dish *adobo*

Being away for 10 months and living alone in a completely different world has taught me a lot of things. I have grown and my **perspective** has changed in ways I never would have imagined. I now can say that I am independent, appreciate my family and friends here more, am open to new ideas, and am more **aggressive** and more confident about myself. Having my own adventure has proven to me that anything is possible and that I can do anything. It was the best time of my life. I will always remember how choosing to go out and discover what the world has in store for me was life-changing, and will be something I will always cherish.

Cause and Effect
How did Elaine's experience as an exchange student affect her personality and her view of life?

---

perspective point of view
aggressive full of energy to go after the things one wants

What Can Journeys Teach?
What did life in Appleton, Wisconsin, teach Elaine about herself? What new experiences did she have? How did these experiences change her? If you could become an exchange student, where would you go? What would you like to learn there? How do you think the experience might change you?

Outward Bound

by Annemarie Brown, Teen Environmental Media Network,
temn@eecom.net

Have you ever pushed yourself to try something you did not think you could do? Challenging experiences can often develop into powerful learning opportunities. In this selection a teenage girl develops the confidence, trust, and strength she needs to overcome problems very different from any she has faced before.

English Coach

Desolation means "loneliness" or "desertion." How would you feel about going to a maze of deserted canyons?

This summer I had the opportunity to travel for 14 days into the depths of Desolation and **Labyrinth** Canyons in the heart of Utah whitewater rafting on the beautiful Green River. Initially, I was not afraid. The best way to describe what I was feeling would be "no emotion." As a socially active fifteen-year-old girl, I didn't want to leave my friends, nor anything with which I was comfortable.

labyrinth a maze made of twisted paths

Outward Bound policy is to have each person step outside the boundaries of that with which they are comfortable. With each step a new fear arises, but also old fears disappear. Outward Bound began 35 years ago. Its mission is to challenge teenagers, as well as adults, to perform tasks that go beyond perceived physical, mental and **emotional** limits so as to **enhance** their belief in themselves and their capabilities.

The trip was truly the first journey of my self-discovery. Challenges and fears stared me in the face everywhere I turned. We had four amazing instructors teaching, guiding, and nurturing us throughout the trip. Their strength of **character** and joy in life were inspiring.

The first challenge, and one of the hardest, was making new friends and hoping they would accept me. In our society, we are judged by our outward appearances. On this trip we were able to glimpse into the souls of those with us. We became open and trusting. "Inward bound" is what it really was; isolated from the outside world, we were there just for each other, with strength, support, and love.

Set a Purpose for Reading
Annemarie says that the trip is a journey of self-discovery, or an opportunity to learn about herself. As you read, look for things that she discovers.

---

emotional related to feelings
enhance add to; increase
character moral firmness

141

Many times we held each other's lives in our hands as we climbed and **rappelled** cliffs. Trust was also a huge factor — if ever that trust was broken you were lost. Love was another factor without which we could not have survived. We adopted our instructors' **motto,** "My love will not fade away."

On several occasions I was faced with challenges I thought I could never conquer. The first was rappelling down a 60-foot cliff! As I stood at the bottom looking up at what I was about to do, it never dawned on me that I was actually going to do it. When my turn came, my instructor showed

me what to do, and courage washed over me as I stepped to the edge. Slowly I looked down — what hit wasn't fear; it was the familiar feeling of "I can't." On a deeper level, I knew I could and I would. Later, standing at the bottom and looking up again, I smiled and said, "Hell, yeah! I can conquer the world!"

rappelled went backwards down a cliff
motto a rule or an idea to live by

What's the Sequence?
What was the first physical challenge that Annemarie faced? Hint: Look for the signal word *first*. Then look for challenges that come later.

142

The journey eventually led us all into the depths of a canyon where we each spent 24 hours alone. We were only allowed to bring a sleeping bag, a gallon of water, some food, and a notebook for writing. Sitting alone on the canyon ledge did not frighten me, and I thought more in that one day than I have in two weeks during my life at home. The journey through my soul was hard; I faced things about myself that I wasn't able to **confront** before.

Looking at the depths of Labyrinth Canyon, I stared into the heart of my fears. Fear stared back through red eyes that, like the colors of the canyon, slowly changed through the day to a glowing yellow. As the moon began to rise over the steep canyon walls, so did my feelings. The flaws I saw within myself shamed me, but the **virtues** I began to see built me up. I felt so strong and beautiful and amazing — but with a sense of **humility** that was also overwhelming. I realized that by accepting myself others would accept me, and by loving myself I am invincible.

Character

What do Annemarie's thoughts about herself tell you about her character? After reading this paragraph, how would you describe her?

confront to face head on
virtues good qualities
humility state of being modest or humble

Labyrinth Canyon

The next morning as the sun rose, I sat in my sleeping bag watching the sunrise and my heart was calm and filled with such strength, clarity and freedom — total **utopia.** I re-entered camp that same morning a different person, with a deep sense of humility, strength and, most important, love.

The last and most brutal part of the journey was when a partner and I carried a heavy (hundred-plus pound) canoe up three miles of steep windy roads. As that canoe sat heavy on my head I was overcome with pain, it felt as if my back would break. We were told before we set out to let our anger carry us, but I had no anger, only a deep hurt — one caused by the pain of self-doubt. I desperately wanted to complete this, only to prove that I could.

The emotional connection between my partner and myself was incredible; in our support for each other we found true inner strength. As we climbed, the pain became too much to bear for us both. We broke down, but we were there for each other. When we reached the top, I was overcome with such joy, such peace, excitement, and love all wrapped into one.

English Coach
Windy has two different pronunciations and meanings. Pronounced \win´· dē \, *windy* means "strongly blowing air." Pronounced \wīn´· dē \, *windy* means "full of twists and turns." Which meaning is intended here?

---

utopia an imaginary place where people enjoy complete happiness

Now, my friends and my experiences are precious memories. Letting go was hugely painful. Returning to 'reality' has been a very difficult transition. But the one thing I have that no one can ever take away is that I now know I can conquer the world — whatever world I might be facing. I hope to call on that experience whenever I feel down or whenever I need love. I know that all my new friends are out there somewhere and they care, they lived it with me. My love will never fade away.

Summarize It

When you are finished reading a selection, it's a good idea to think about what you learned from it. In your own words, try to tell the most important ideas. Use the questions *Who? What? Where? When? Why?* and *How?* to help you recall ideas.

What Can Journeys Teach?

What did Annemarie learn from her journey? What did she learn about her physical abilities? What did she discover about her inner self? Do you think Annemarie was more challenged by the physical journey or the mental one? Where would you go to challenge yourself physically and mentally? What might this journey teach you about yourself?

The Flying Fool

by Thomas Fleming

Today thousands of airplanes fly across the oceans every day. But in 1927 no one had ever flown across the Atlantic Ocean. Most people thought that it could not be done. Charles Lindbergh proved them wrong when he made a dangerous nonstop flight from New York to Paris.

In 1927, airplane travel was still something new. No one had ever even flown an airplane from the United States to mainland Europe.

One New York hotel owner wanted to challenge some brave pilot to do so. He offered a $25,000 prize to the first **aviator** who flew nonstop across the Atlantic between New York and Paris.

aviator a person who flies airplanes

Character
What kind of person would try to be the first to fly across the Atlantic for $25,000? Think of words that might describe this person.

146

Lindbergh poses in front of his plane, the *Spirit of St. Louis,* before his historic flight.

Charles A. Lindbergh was a 25-year-old air-mail pilot from Minnesota. He was planning to fly the 3,636 miles alone, in a single-engine plane called the *Spirit of St. Louis.* Newspapers nicknamed him "The Flying Fool." How could he compete?

To succeed, Lindbergh decided the plane had to be as light as possible. He **supervised** every step of its construction in San Diego, California. He **eliminated** the windshield and put two fuel tanks in the nose. He reduced his equipment to a minimum: a 10-pound rubber raft, a knife, some flares, a flashlight, a fishing line and hook, some chocolate **rations.** The main thing the plane would carry besides the 170-pound pilot was 451 gallons of gas.

supervised directed and managed
eliminated got rid of; removed
rations limited amounts of food

Make Inferences
Reread the list of emergency equipment that Lindbergh took with him. What inferences can you make about the dangers that Lindbergh thought he might face? How would the equipment have helped him?

Up, Up and Away

Storms over the Atlantic delayed Lindbergh for almost two weeks. On Thursday, May 19, the weather **bureau** reported it was clearing over the ocean but rain and wind would continue in New York. Lindbergh went to bed in a Long Island hotel, not far from where his plane was waiting. He could not sleep. He got up at 2:30 a.m. and drove through the rain to the airfield, where a big crowd was waiting for him.

Excitement grew as mechanics hauled the plane to nearby Roosevelt Field, which had a longer runway. "It was more like a funeral **procession** than the beginning of a flight to Paris," Lindbergh later recalled.

Lindbergh sat in the plane trying to decide whether to take off, while the rain fell around him. Not until daybreak, after reading more weather reports, did Lindbergh decide to go. Now came the real suspense. Could the *Spirit of St. Louis* get off the ground, loaded with 451 gallons of gasoline?

Compare and Contrast
How might the plane trip to Roosevelt Field have been like a funeral procession? Hint: How do you think Lindbergh felt as he watched the plane draw near?

bureau an organization that collects or provides information
procession a line of cars that moves in a formal way

Lindbergh had never tested the plane with that much fuel in its tanks. Halfway down the runway, Lindbergh still wasn't sure the plane would make it into the air. Seconds now to decide, he warned himself. The wrong decision meant a crash, probably in flames.

He pulled the stick back firmly. The wheels left the ground. Then they touched down again. He was almost at flying speed. It was too late to stop now. There was a web of telephone wires on poles at the end of the runway. He had to clear them.

Water splashed against the plane as it tore through a big puddle on the runway. The plane lifted off again — and came back down with the left wing low. Lindbergh leveled it as the plane hit another puddle. Airborne again, he let the wheels touch once more. "A little bow to earth, a gesture of **humility**," he called it.

The next time, the *Spirit of St. Louis* stayed in the air and cleared the telephone lines by 20 feet. The Flying Fool was on his way to Paris.

humility the state of being modest or humble

Narrative or Informational?
As the writer describes the plane's takeoff, is the style of writing narrative or informational? How do you know? Hint: Narrative writing tells a story. Informational writing gives facts.

Almost done with his long journey, Lindbergh flies over the Eiffel Tower in Paris on May 19, 1927.

Can He Stay Awake?

When Lindbergh took off, he had not slept for 24 hours. Many people doubted he could stay awake for his lonely flight, which would take an estimated 36 hours. By this time the whole world was watching. Ships reported seeing him off Cape Cod heading toward Nova Scotia. He flew low, sometimes only 10 feet above the water, to save gas and keep his mind alert.

Nova Scotia was the first test of his **navigation.** Lindbergh was relieved to find he was only six miles off course. But after eight hours, his eyes began to feel "dry and hard as stones." He forced them open then squeezed them shut again and again.

---

navigation   process of plotting or directing the course of an airplane or ship

Think About It
Sometimes imagining yourself in a situation can help you understand what a character is going through. Why do you think flying low helped Lindbergh keep his mind alert?

Lindbergh lands in London after a successful Atlantic crossing in May 1927.

Night fell as he flew over Newfoundland. Below him ghostly white icebergs appeared by the dozens. Realizing he had a tailwind, which would increase his air speed, Lindbergh decided he had enough gasoline to climb to 10,000 feet. Suddenly huge clouds loomed ahead. It became very cold in the cockpit. Lindbergh stuck his hand out the side window and felt sleet sting his skin. He grabbed a flashlight and saw ice forming on one of the wing **struts.** If it formed on the wings he was doomed. Wind lashed the plane. The two compasses on which he depended for navigation stopped working. At one point a fierce gust turned the plane completely around. Abruptly the clouds separated, and up ahead Lindbergh saw moonlight. As he crossed the halfway mark of his flight, the ice vanished from his struts. His compasses began working again.

After 17 hours in the air, Lindbergh's body ached, his face burned. He was desperate for sleep. He dived low enough to let spray from whitecaps **douse** his face. Another time, he let light rain blow into the cockpit to keep him awake. At one point, he looked down and saw a whole continent off his left wing — a **mirage.**

English Coach
The compound word *tailwind* is made up of *tail,* which means "the back end of something," and *wind,* which means "air that moves." What does *tailwind* mean? What other compound words can you find in this paragraph?

---

struts rods that are used to support something
douse to throw water or another liquid onto
mirage a vision of an object that is not really there

Suddenly he saw fishing boats below him. On one he saw a man staring up at him. Lindbergh spiraled down and shouted: "Which way is Ireland?" Getting no answer, he flew on. He began to see gulls. More land loomed ahead. It was Ireland! He was only three miles off course!

Next Stop, Paris

Lindbergh's need for sleep vanished. Hope surged through his body. Minutes later, the *Spirit of St. Louis*'s motor started coughing **ominously.** Lindbergh prepared for a crash landing.

Then he realized one of the fuel tanks in the nose had run dry. He had forgotten to switch to his reserve tank. He turned a valve and the motor resumed its steady rhythm.

---

ominously in a threatening or scary way

Problems and Solutions
What problem occurred with the motor of Lindbergh's plane? How did he solve this problem?

WELCOME LINDBERGH
NEW YORK TO PARIS
33·HRS· 21·MIN·
19 27

When Lindbergh returned to the United States, New York City held a parade to honor him.

As the sun went down, Lindbergh crossed the English Channel into France. He had now flown 3,500 miles, breaking the world's distance record. For the first time he felt hungry. He gnawed on one of five sandwiches a friend had given him before takeoff. He could barely swallow each bite. His body was close to collapsing.

As Lindbergh neared Paris, he climbed to 4,000 feet. Below him he saw the lights of the city. He circled above the **illuminated** Eiffel Tower and after momentary confusion found Le Bourget Airport. He fastened his safety belt, cut his air speed and made a perfect landing in the middle of the runway. It was 10:24 p.m. Paris time — 33 1/2 hours since Lindbergh left New York.

illuminated lit up

Summarize It
Tell in your own words the important facts about Lindbergh's journey. Remember to answer the questions *Who? What? Where? When? Why?* and *How?*

What Can Journeys Teach?

What did the world of aviation learn from Lindbergh's journey? What did Lindbergh learn about himself? What other people do you know of who did things that no one had ever done before? What did they do? If you could be the first person to do something important, what would it be? What might you learn from this journey?

JOURNEY INTO THE WEST

About 200 years ago, Lewis and Clark led a group of explorers on a historic journey to learn about the West. They recorded details about plants, animals, and places that most people had never seen before. No one knew if it was even possible to reach the Pacific Ocean and return. There was only one way to find out.

English Coach
Handful can mean "as many as a hand can hold" or "a small number." What does *handful* mean here? How do you know?

In 1802 the western border of the United States reached only as far as the Mississippi River. The country was mostly wilderness or farmland, with only a handful of cities. President Thomas Jefferson wanted to help American businesses grow, and he wanted to increase trade with the native peoples in the West. He thought he could accomplish both goals by sending an **expedition** to explore the West.

Jefferson hoped to find a way to travel through this **uncharted** land entirely by boat, using the rivers as a kind of highway through forests and mountain ranges. He had more plans for the trip too.

---

expedition a journey made for a specific purpose
uncharted not yet mapped or explored

The route that Lewis and Clark took through the Louisiana Territory

He wanted to open trading posts along the rivers and seaports on the West Coast. But there was one big problem with Jefferson's dream. At that time, the **territory** beyond the Mississippi River was divided into colonies belonging to Britain, Spain, Russia, and France.

In 1803 Jefferson bought France's portion of the territory. This new addition, called the Louisiana Purchase, extended from the Mississippi River to the Rocky Mountains and from the Gulf of Mexico to the Canadian border.

Jefferson could not wait to learn about the land he had bought. He chose two intelligent and **resourceful** men, Meriwether Lewis and William Clark, to lead an expedition through the West.

What Do You Know?
Trace the boundaries of the Louisiana Purchase on the map with your finger. What states now make up that territory?

---

territory a large area of land
resourceful skillful and clever in solving problems

In May 1804, Lewis, Clark, and about forty-two men — plus Lewis's dog, Seaman — boarded a **keelboat** and two canoes at the mouth of the Missouri River and began their journey. As they went along, the Corps of Discovery met many different native tribes. They drew maps and took **specimens** of the land. They recorded in their journal all of the important details: the people they met, the decisions they made, and the adventures they had.

In October the men stopped in what is now North Dakota. They built a fort and settled in for the winter near where the Mandan Indians lived. There they met a fur trapper named Charbonneau and his wife Sacagawea, a Shoshone. The pair joined the explorers to serve as **interpreters** and guides.

In the spring, the expedition continued up the Missouri River in six canoes. After passing the Yellowstone and Musselshell rivers, the explorers came to dangerous rapids. Captain Lewis wrote:

---

keelboat a shallow boat that people move with poles and oars
specimens small amounts taken as samples
interpreters people who help speakers of different languages to communicate

English Coach
As an adjective, *rapid* means "very fast." When you add an *-s*, you get *rapids*, which is a noun that means "a part of a river where the currents run very fast." Have you ever seen rapids? Where?

May 31, 1805

The rapids are troublesome and difficult to pass. Our rope broke and we were in danger of turning over in the canoe. Our men have hard work going up this part of the Missouri because they have to walk barefooted in the water on slippery rocks and through stiff mud, since their moccasins come off in the mud.

A little farther along, the river forked north and south. The captains were unsure which way to go. Their decision to go south turned out to be the correct one. However, soon they came to several waterfalls. While **investigating** how to proceed, Captain Lewis had a scare:

English Coach
Forked is a verb that means "split into different directions." In your own words, tell what you think the phrase *a fork in the road* means.

June 14, 1805

A large bear crept within twenty steps before I discovered him. My gun was not loaded and there was nowhere to hide from this monster until I could recharge. He came at me open mouthed and full speed. I ran into the water about waist deep and faced him with my espontoon [sharp-pointed staff]. He suddenly turned and retreated.

---

investigating looking into something thoroughly to find out facts or details

Problems and Solutions

What problem did the waterfalls and the Rocky Mountains create for the explorers? How did they solve this problem?

The waterfalls and the Rocky Mountains made it impossible to continue by water, so the captains decided to build a wagon to carry the canoes. For weeks they were burdened by mosquitoes, hot sun, and cold rain. At times they were able to travel by river. Sacagawea told them that farther along they would meet the Shoshones, her own tribe. Then the captains could buy horses to carry them over the mountains.

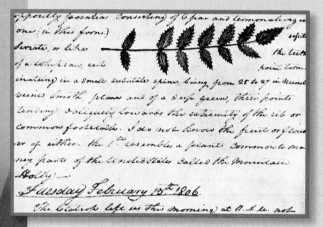

When they finally met the Shoshones, Sacagawea was overjoyed to find her brother, Cameahwait, who was now the chief. The Shoshones sold horses to the captains and explained how to get to "the stinking lake," which is what the Shoshones called the ocean. Lewis wrote in the journal:

August 14, 1805
The chief drew the river on which we now are and placed two branches just above us. He made it empty into a large river, … Here he placed heaps of sand on each side, which he said represented the vast mountains of rock covered with snow through which the river passed. The chief said this river ran a long way toward the setting sun and finally lost itself in a great lake of water that tasted bad and where white men lived.

In the mountains, snow and a lack of food slowed the men down considerably. They almost starved, but the Nez Percé gave them food and helped them build new canoes. The Nez Percé showed them the way to the Snake River. Many of the men in the Corps of Discovery were sick and weary, but they managed to travel on. Clark wrote in the journal:

Cause and Effect
What effects did the snow and lack of food have on the explorers?

> September 24, 1805
> Captain Lewis scarcely able to ride on a gentle horse furnished by the chief. Several men so unwell they had to lie on the side of the trail for some time.

The men braved more rapids on the Snake River and also on the mighty Columbia River. At last the Corps of Discovery reached the Pacific Ocean. Clark wrote:

> November 7, 1805
> Great joy in camp. We are in view of the ocean, which we have been so long anxious to see.

Sacagawea guiding the explorers through the Rocky Mountains

The Corps of Discovery settled in for the winter. They had traveled about 3,700 miles. On March 23, 1806, they started back up the Columbia River and into the mountains. This time they decided to split up to find a better route. Clark traveled swiftly, thanks to Sacagawea's directions, and then canoed down the Yellowstone River. Lewis returned to the waterfalls and then to the fork in the Missouri River to explore north. Then the two teams met up again. On September 23 the Corps of Discovery landed back in St. Louis — two and a half years after they had set off.

The expedition did not find a river passage to the Pacific, but they learned much about the West and its **inhabitants.** Their maps and journals provide a record of **fascinating** people, wildlife, plants, and places that most people at that time had never seen or even heard of.

inhabitants people and animals that live in a particular place
fascinating extremely interesting

Ask Questions

After reading a selection like this, it's a good idea to ask yourself *Who? What? Where? When? Why?* and *How?* questions to be sure you remember all of the important facts. If there's something you don't remember, you can go back and reread until you find it.

What Can Journeys Teach?

Where did Lewis and Clark's journey take them? What did they learn from the journey? Do you think the country would be different if Lewis and Clark hadn't made this journey? How? If you could journey to an unexplored place, where would you go? Why?

How Does Nature Touch Lives?

Nature is all around you. It is the water you drink, the air you breathe, and the food you eat. It is in your clothes and in your home.

Nature can be as constant as the way night follows day or the way the seasons change. Or it can be as surprising as a gust of wind or a sudden rain.

Each selection in this unit focuses on a single part of nature. As you read, think about the role nature plays in the selection. Then ask yourself, how does nature touch lives?

Whirlwind Survivors
Heartland residents recount tales of tornadoes, terror

by James A. Fussell, *The Kansas City Star,* May 4, 2002

Sometimes nature touches lives in unforgettable ways. Who could ever forget the sight of a tornado ripping through homes, tearing off roofs, and picking up cars? Tornadoes often strike without warning and change lives forever in minutes. Read on to find out what happened to two people who met tornadoes head-on.

Think About It

If something confuses you when you read, reading on may help. Here, for example, you might wonder what the author is describing. Keep reading. When does the author name what he is describing?

They can sound like a freight train or a thousand jet engines, or they can be eerily silent.

They can form out of greenish-black skies or pop out of nowhere during an otherwise delightful day.

They can be monsters or **pipsqueaks,** hit farm homes or big cities, jump rivers, climb hillsides, and come anytime of the day or night.

---

pipsqueaks small or unimportant persons or things

Despite advances in weather forecasting, there's simply no **blueprint** for how or when a tornado will strike. But there is one thing about a twister you can count on, those who have experienced them say: If it comes for you, you will never be the same.

Context Clues

Find the word *twister* in this paragraph. Use clues in the sentences around the word to tell what it means.

As tornado season starts again, we asked two generations of twister **survivors** — from Pomona Lake, Kansas, and Ruskin Heights, Kansas — to share their stories.

Think tornadoes won't strike where you live? So did they.

Pomona Lake, 1978

There was no angry black sky, and no pounding hail. The relatively small tornado that **capsized** the *Whippoorwill* showboat on Pomona Lake literally came out of the blue. Lawrence Stadel, who owned the Lighthouse Bay Marina at the time, can never forget that day.

"I was standing on the north edge of the dock thinking, 'Gee, the weather sure is nice. The wind has finally gone down,'" he said.

---

blueprint carefully worked-out plan or model
survivors people who have lived through an accident or a disaster
capsized turned upside-down in water

Three minutes later, the calm was shattered by a frantic voice on a speeding boat.

"Tornado!"

Stadel turned, and in the distance saw a small finger of swirling water splashing on the surface of the lake. He was impressed by its speed but figured it was too small to be dangerous.

But as he soon learned, even small tornadoes can be deadly.

The small spout headed straight for the *Whippoorwill*, a dinner-theater boat loaded with more than 50 people. The boat's captain turned the boat and tried to make it to shore. Before he could, the swirling winds hit the boat **broadside** and flipped it over.

The twister lasted only eight minutes, but that was more than enough. Passengers tumbled into the water, and many were trapped under the boat.

Stadel climbed in a 28-foot **pontoon boat** and raced to the scene. Dozens of frantic survivors jumped on board until the craft was overloaded. At least he would get them to safety.

Or would he?

---

broadside directly from the side
pontoon boat a flat-bottomed boat

Predict
What do you predict will happen to the "small finger of swirling water"? What might it do? What will Stadel do? Use information that you have already read to help you predict what may happen next.

Context Clues
What does *craft* mean in this paragraph? What context clues helped you determine the meaning?

The showboat *Whippoorwill*, capsized by a tornado on June 17, 1978

Just as he was pulling into the mouth of the marina's **cove,** he saw another tornado about a mile and a half away. It was nearly 10 times as large as the first one, kicking up dust and heading straight toward them. Luckily, the tornado veered south and missed them.

With no time to lose, Stadel, a veteran diver, grabbed his gear and headed back. People told Stadel they heard pounding under the boat.

He dove into the murky blackness and felt around with his hands. He found one man trapped in a small air pocket in the boiler room.

"Grab ahold of my foot and hang on," he told him.

After reaching the surface, he went back to look for more, but had no luck. Then, 30 minutes later, someone heard a noise.

English Coach
Veteran means "skilled and experienced in a certain activity." What do you think an army veteran is?

cove small, sheltered area of water off of a larger body of water

Draw Conclusions
What conclusions can you draw about how people act when they are afraid for their lives? Think about the actions of the young man who is almost out of air.

Stadel dove back in. Suddenly, near the engine room, someone grabbed his hand. Then the person pulled his face mask off, almost **dislodging** his mouthpiece. By the size of his arm, he was a young man, Stadel said. And judging by the intensity of his desperation he was almost out of air.

Stadel grabbed the young man, dove down beyond the boat's edge and brought him to the surface.

Thanks to Stadel, the men joined dozens of others who survived the *Whippoorwill* tornado.

Sixteen others did not.

Ruskin Heights, 1957

After many years, the muddy monster that swept Louis Mannen's home from the face of the earth is still as real as if it were raging right in front of him.

---

dislodging moving or forcing out of position

Ruskin Heights High School after the tornado

It was large, black, and evil. It blew through buildings like they were made of cardboard and hurled concrete like **confetti.**

On May 20, 1957, Mannen, then principal of the old Palmer Junior High School in Independence, was late coming home from work. After a parent-teacher conference he climbed into his dark-green Plymouth and drove south down Noland Road. The sky was unusually dark. The day before, strong winds had blown off his driver's side windshield wiper. Fearing rain, he pulled over to move the remaining wiper to the driver's side. That's when he saw it — and heard it.

It was roaring across the road in the distance, a loud and angry killer, spitting out boards and concrete blocks and ripping the roofs off nearby houses. Worse, it was heading straight for his Ruskin Heights neighborhood where his wife, 3-year-old son and 3-month-old daughter had no basement in which to take cover.

As it passed, his future flashed in front of him.

He returned to his car and tried to go home. But cars had streamed into the path of the tornado's destruction, snarling traffic. Stuck along U.S. 71, he could wait no longer.

---

confetti small pieces of paper thrown into the air at parties or parades

Visualize It
How do the phrases "blew through buildings like they were made of cardboard" and "hurled concrete like confetti" help you picture the tornado? What do the images tell about the tornado?

Cause and Effect
What causes Mannen to get out of his car and begin to run?

He got out of his car and began to run, past destruction and **debris,** past horror and pain. When he got to his neighborhood his heart sunk — there was no neighborhood. Frantic, he looked around, calling for his wife and his kids. Where his house used to be he saw a sickening sight — the flat concrete slab his home was built on — and nothing else.

Just then a neighbor gave him a piece of good news in the midst of all the bad. His family was not among the dozens who died as a direct result of the storm. A **Good Samaritan** had taken them away to get some help.

But where? He spent the rest of the day trying to find them. Finally, at midnight, he found them at a Grandview hospital. Seeing them alive was all he could have hoped for.

---

debris remains of something broken or destroyed
Good Samaritan person who unselfishly helps others

"It was a happy reunion," he said.

They were fortunate to be alive. With no basement they had braved the storm in a hallway. Somehow, Mannen's wife was able to keep the twister from sucking her baby out of her arms. Her 3-year-old was another story. Swirling winds picked him up, blew his pajamas off and deposited him in the front yard. As the tornado roared away he had two black eyes, a sliver of wood sticking out of the back of his head, and gravel **embedded** in his neck.

English Coach
The adjective *brave* means "full of courage." Here the word *braved* is a verb. What do you think the verb *braved* means? Have you ever braved a tough situation?

He sat in the dirt and debris and cried: "My house is broken!"

More than 40 of their neighbors didn't survive.

After the storm Mannen moved to Independence, where he lives today — in a home with a basement.

embedded fixed firmly into something

How Does Nature Touch Lives?

Tornadoes touched the lives of both Stadel and Mannen. How were their experiences the same? How were they different? How may other types of weather touch lives? Has your life ever been affected by the weather? How?

From the water we drink to the lakes and oceans we swim in, water is a part of nature that touches our lives every day. Large bodies of water can be beautiful and peaceful, but they can also produce dangerous waves and rip currents. As this essay and poem show, water demands respect.

Chicago Waters

by Susan Power

My mother used to say that by the time I was an old woman, Lake Michigan would be the size of a silver dollar. She pinched her index finger with her thumb to show me the pitiful **dimensions.**

"People will gather around the tiny lake, what's left of it, and cluck over a spoonful of water," she told me.

I learned to squint at the 1967 shoreline until I had carved away the structures and roads built on landfill, and could imagine the lake and its city as my mother found them in 1942 when she arrived in Chicago. I say *the lake and its city* rather than *the city and its lake* because my mother taught me another secret: the city of Chicago belongs to Lake Michigan.

dimensions measurements of an area

More Information

The Great Fire of 1871 destroyed much of the city of Chicago. Workers pushed the waste from the fire into Lake Michigan. Then the city was rebuilt on top of this landfill. Since then, roads, a football stadium, and many parks have been built on the landfill.

When my mother watches the water from her lakeside apartment building, she still sucks in her breath. "You have to respect the power of that lake," she tells me. "You see, no matter how much the city fathers tried to tame that water, it goes wild whenever it wants to. So you respect this powerful being."

And I do now. I do.

I was fifteen years old when I learned that the lake did not love me or hate me, but could claim me, nevertheless. I was showing off for a boy, my best friend, Tommy, who lived in the same building. He usually accompanied me when I went for a swim, but on this particular day he decided the water was too choppy. I always preferred the lake when it was **agitated** because its temperature warmed, transforming it into a kind of Jacuzzi.

Predict
The narrator says she learned that the lake did not love her or hate her, but could claim her. What do you predict will happen to the narrator to teach her this lesson?

---

agitated shaken up violently

To help you picture
the scene, the narrator
compares the ladder
to the entrance to
the deep end of a
swimming pool. How
does this comparison
help you picture the
place where she enters
the water?

Tommy is right, I thought, once I saw the looming swells that had looked so unimpressive from the twelfth floor. Waves crashed against the breakwater wall and the metal ladder that led into and out of the lake like the entrance to the deep end of a swimming pool.

I shouldn't do this, I told myself, but I noticed Tommy watching me from his first-floor window. "I'm not afraid," I said to him under my breath. "I bet you think that I'll chicken out just because I'm a girl."

It had been a hot summer of dares, some foolish, some **benign.** Sense was clearly wanting. I took a deep breath and leaped off the wall into the **turmoil,** since the ladder was under attack. How did I think I would get out of the water? I hadn't thought that far. I bobbed to the surface and was instantly slapped in the face. I was beaten by water, smashed under again and again, until I began choking because I couldn't catch my breath.

**Problems and
Solutions**
What problem does the
narrator begin to have
after she jumps into the
water? As you read, look
for how she solves her
problems.

---

benign   not harmful
turmoil   great confusion; in this case, rolling and choppy waves

Waves crash against the shore south of downtown Chicago.

I'm going to die now, I realized, and my heart filled with sorrow for my mother, who had already lost a husband and would now lose a daughter. I fought the waves, struggled to reach the air and the light, the sound of breakers swelling in my ears, unnaturally loud, like the noise of judgment day. *Here we go,* I thought.

Then I surprised myself, becoming unusually calm. I managed a quick gasp of breath and plunged to the bottom of the lake, where the water was a little quieter. I swam to the beach next door, remaining on the lake floor until I reached shallow waters. I burst to the surface then, my lungs burning, and it took me nearly five minutes to walk fifteen feet, knocked off balance as I was by waves that sucked at my legs. This beach now belongs to my mother and the other **shareholders** in her building, property recently purchased and attached to their existing lot.

---

shareholders people who own part of something

English Coach
Breakers are "waves that crash against the shore." Can you imagine the sound that breakers make?

Susan Power

But in 1977 it was owned by someone else, and a barbed-wire fence separated the properties. I ended my misadventure by managing to climb over the sharp wire.

I remained downstairs until I stopped shaking. Tommy no longer watched me from his window, bored by my private games, unaware of the danger. I didn't tell my mother what had happened until hours later. I was angry at myself for being so foolish, so careless with my life, but I was never for a moment angry at the lake. I didn't come to fear it either, though it is a mighty force that drops 923 feet in its deepest heart. I understood that it struck **indifferently;** I was neither target nor friend. My life was my own affair, to lose or to save. Once I stopped struggling with the great lake, I flowed through it, and was **expelled** from its **hectic** mouth.

---

indifferently without preference for anyone or anything
expelled pushed out
hectic marked by intense activity or confusion

Booming Ground

by Ray Gonzalez

We sit in your boat and
you tell us how you lost your
anchor in the **booming ground**
when you sailed to Alaska,
how you found out the man who sails is
the man who stays ahead of the sea,
on top of the **gale** that blows him
into deep **fathoms** of darkness.

---

booming ground a body of water where people collect,
sort, or store logs
gale very strong wind
fathoms units of length equal to six feet, used mainly to
measure depth in the ocean

Think About It
You often have to reread
poetry and use what you
know to figure out the
image or message of the
poem. Use what you
know about logging, the
business of cutting trees
for lumber, to picture
the booming ground.
Use what you know
about storms at sea
to understand why a
sailor must "stay ahead
of the sea."

We sit on the pier and watch
the ducks dive for food,
disappear for minutes,
then suddenly pop up for air.
If there is this kind of
motion in the heart,
the boat rocks with
its exhausted rhythm.

Without time to take us sailing,

I wonder why you brought us here,

but sitting in your small boat,

I come closer to water without fear.

I picture you sailing, alone,

into the sound, absorbed in

gray mist that hides you from yourself

because, as the gulls interrupt and

larger boats leave the docks,

I know you are telling us

the sailor who knows where

he is bound expects

too much from the sea.

English Coach
Here, *sound* means
"a long body of water."
What is another meaning
of *sound*?

English Coach
Here, *bound* means
"going to a certain place,"
as in a ship that is *bound*
for South America.

How Does Nature Touch Lives?

Nature can touch lives with one event, or it can affect
lives over many years. In these selections, which
narrator's life was touched by a single event? Which
narrator was affected by a lifetime of experiences with
water? What lessons did each learn from his or her
experiences? What lessons has nature taught you?

The Rain Came

by Grace A. Ogot

> Every culture includes tales and legends in which nature plays an important part. This selection tells the story of an African village where rain is very important. When rain does not come for a long time, it is up to Oganda to save her village.

The time for her departure was drawing near and each minute was precious. It was a day's journey to the lake. She was to walk all night, passing through the great forest. But nothing could touch her, not even the **denizens** of the forest. She was already **anointed** with sacred oil. From the time Oganda received the sad news, she had expected Osinda to appear any moment. But he was not there. A relative told her that Osinda was away on a private visit. Oganda realized that she would never see her dear one again.

Think About It

As you read, stop from time to time to check your understanding. Here, for example, you might ask: Why is Oganda going to the lake? What sad news did she receive? Reading on will often answer your questions.

---

denizens people, plants, or animals that live in a certain area
anointed made pure by applying oil

In the afternoon the whole village stood at the gate to say good-bye and to see her for the last time. Her mother wept on her neck for a long time. The great chief in a **mourning** skin came to the gate barefooted and mingled with the people — a simple father in grief. He took off his wrist bracelet and put it on his daughter's wrist, saying, "You will always live among us. The spirit of our forefathers is with you."

Tongue-tied and unbelieving, Oganda stood there before the people. She had nothing to say. She looked at her home once more. She could hear her heart beating so painfully within her. All her childhood plans were dew again. She looked at her weeping mother and whispered, "Whenever you want to see me, always look at the sunset. I will be there."

Context Clues
Oganda is described as *tongue-tied.* Use context clues to figure out the meaning of this word. How could the two words in *tongue-tied* help you figure out its meaning?

---

mourning   showing grief for the dead

179

Visualize It

Imagine that you live in Oganda's village. Describe what you see as you watch Oganda walk away. What words and phrases from the text help you visualize the scene?

Oganda turned southwards to start her trek to the lake. Her parents, relatives, friends and admirers stood at the gate and watched her go. Her beautiful, slender figure grew smaller and smaller till she mingled with the thin dry trees in the forest.

As Oganda walked the lonely path that wound its way in the wilderness she sang a song and her own voice kept her company.

"The ancestors have said Oganda must die;
The daughter of the chief must be sacrificed.
When the lake monster feeds on my flesh,
The people will have rain;
Yes, the rain will come down in **torrents.**
The wind will blow, the thunder will roar.
And the floods will wash away the sandy beaches
When the daughter of the chief dies in the lake.
My age-group has consented,
My parents have **consented,**
So have my friends and relatives;
Let Oganda die to give us rain.
My age-group are young and ripe,
Ripe for womanhood and motherhood;
But Oganda must die young,
Oganda must sleep with the ancestors.
Yes, rain will come down in torrents."

---

torrents heavy rains; downpours
consented given approval

What Do You Know?
Oganda is willing to sacrifice her life so that rain will come. What other tales do you know in which people make sacrifices or do brave deeds to please monsters, spirits, or gods?

The red rays of the setting sun embraced Oganda, and she looked like a burning candle in the wilderness.

The people who came to hear her sad song were touched by her beauty. But they all said the same thing: "If it is to save the people, if it is to give us rain, then be not afraid. Your name will for ever live among us."

At midnight Oganda was tired and weary. She could walk no more. She sat under a big tree and, having sipped water from her **calabash,** she rested her head on the tree trunk and slept.

When she woke up in the morning the sun was high in the sky. After walking for many hours she reached the tong, a strip of land that separated the inhabited part of the country from the sacred place — kar lamo. No **lay** man could enter this place and come out alive — only those who had direct contact with the spirits and the Almighty were allowed to enter his holy of holies. But Oganda had to pass through this sacred land on her way to the lake, which she had to reach at sunset.

Make Inferences
The people tell Oganda that her name will for ever live among them. What can you infer about the way that the people of Oganda's village honor their important ancestors?

Context Clues
Use context clues to figure out what the phrase *his holy of holies* means. Hint: What place is no lay person allowed to enter?

calabash a large gourd, or fruit with a tough skin, that can be used to make bowls or containers
lay not a religious leader

A large crowd gathered to see her for the last time. Her voice was now hoarse and painful but there was no need to worry any more. Soon she would not have to sing. The crowd looked at Oganda **sympathetically,** mumbling words she could not hear. But none of them pleaded for her life. As Oganda opened the gate a child, a young child, broke loose from the crowd and ran toward her. The child took a small ear-ring from her sweaty hands and gave it to Oganda, saying, "When you reach the world of the dead, give this ear-ring to my sister. She died last week. She forgot this ring." Oganda, taken aback by this strange request, took the little ring and handed her precious water and food to the child. She did not need them now.

Draw Conclusions
Why does Oganda give her water and food to the child? Hint: Why does she not need them anymore?

sympathetically in a way that shares the feelings of another

Oganda did not know whether to laugh or cry. She had heard mourners sending their love to their sweethearts, long dead, but this idea of sending gifts was new to her.

Oganda held her breath as she crossed the barrier to enter the sacred land. She looked **appealingly** at the crowd but there was no response. Their minds were too **preoccupied** with their own survival. Rain was the precious medicine they were longing for, and the sooner Oganda could get to her destination the better.

A strange feeling possessed the princess as she picked her way in the sacred land. There were strange noises that often startled her and her first reaction was to take to her heels. But she remembered that she had to fulfill the wish of her people. She was exhausted, but the path was still winding. Then suddenly the path ended on sandy land. The water had retreated miles away from the shore, leaving a wide stretch of sand. Beyond this was the vast expanse of water.

Oganda felt afraid. She wanted to picture the size and shape of the monster, but fear would not let her.

English Coach

The expression *take to one's heels* means "to run away." What do you think the expression *drag one's heels* means?

---

appealingly in a way that calls for help or attention
preoccupied focused on

The people did not talk about it, nor did the crying children who were silenced at the mention of its name. The sun was still up but it was no longer hot. For a long time Oganda walked ankle-deep in the sand. She was exhausted and longed desperately for her calabash of water. As she moved on she had a strange feeling that something was following her. Was it the monster? Her hair stood erect and a cold **paralyzing** feeling ran along her spine. She looked behind, sideways and in front, but there was nothing except a cloud of dust.

paralyzing   making someone or something unable to feel or move

Think About It
Have you ever been afraid of an unknown monster? Have you ever had a "hair-raising" or "spine-tingling" experience? Answering these questions can help you understand how Oganda feels.

How Does Nature Touch Lives?

How do you think this story ends? Does the lake monster eat Oganda? Is her life spared? Does your life depend on nature as much as the lives of the people in Oganda's village do? Why or why not? How does nature provide for you?

When Plague Strikes

by James Cross Giblin

The Black Plague was a disease that swept across Asia and Europe in the mid-1300s. By 1400, the plague had killed 20 to 30 million people. What caused this disease to spread so quickly and touch so many lives? Today we know that the plague was caused by natural events. But how was nature to blame?

Narrative or Informational?
Is the writing style of this selection narrative or informational? What clues helped you decide?

Early in 1347, a mysterious disease attacked people living near the Black Sea in what is now southern Ukraine. Its victims suffered from headaches, felt weak and tired, and staggered when they tried to walk.

By the third day, the **lymph nodes** in the sufferers' **groins,** or occasionally their armpits, began to swell.

---

lymph nodes body parts that supply white blood cells and help fight sickness
groins areas of the body where the legs join together

Soon they reached the size of hens' eggs. These swellings became known as buboes, from the Greek word for groin, *boubon*. They gave the disease its official name: the bubonic plague.

The victim's heart beat wildly as it tried to pump blood through the swollen tissues. The **nervous system** started to collapse, causing dreadful pain and bizarre movements of the arms and legs. Then, as death neared, the mouth gaped open and the skin blackened from **internal** bleeding. The end usually came on the fifth day.

A young man with the bubonic plague

Within weeks of the first reported cases, hundreds of people in the Black Sea region had sickened and died. Those who survived were terrified. Like the citizens of Athens at the time of the Plague, they had no medicines with which to fight the disease. As it continued to spread, their fear changed to frustration, and then to anger. Someone — some outsider — must be responsible for bringing this **calamity** upon them.

More Information
The city of Athens, Greece, was struck by a mysterious plague in the fifth century B.C. Even today doctors and other experts do not agree on what caused this plague.

nervous system the body system that includes the brain, spinal cord, and nerves
internal located inside
calamity something that causes great distress or suffering

English Coach
Here, *candidates* means "people likely to to have caused something to happen." What were the Italian traders likely to have caused? What other meaning of *candidates* do you know?

The most likely candidates were the Italian traders who operated in the region. They bartered Italian goods for the silks and spices that came over the **caravan** routes from the Far East, then shipped the Eastern merchandise on to Italy. Although many of the traders had lived in the region for years, they were still thought of as being different. For one thing, they were Christians, while most of the natives were Muslims.

Deciding the Italians were to blame for the **epidemic,** the natives gathered an army and prepared to attack their trading post. The Italians fled to a fortress they had built on the coast of the Black Sea. There the natives **besieged** them until the dread disease broke out in the Muslim army.

The natives were forced to withdraw. But before they did — according to one account — they gave the Italians a taste of the agony their people had been suffering. They loaded catapults with the bodies of some of their dead soldiers and hurled them over the high walls into the fortress. By doing so, they hoped to infect the Italians with the plague.

Predict
Think about what you have read so far. What do you think will happen to the Italian traders? As you read, continue to check your predictions and make new ones.

---

caravan a group that travels together, especially through a desert
epidemic disease that spreads rapidly to many people
besieged surrounded with armed forces

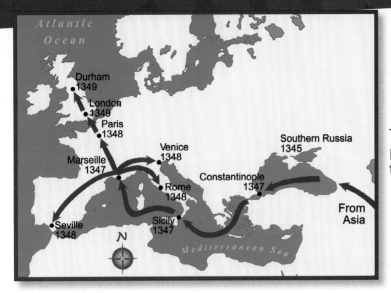

The path of the bubonic plague as it traveled throughout Europe

As fast as the bodies landed, the Italians dumped them into the sea. However, they did not move quickly enough, for the disease had already taken hold among them. In a panic, the traders loaded three ships and set sail for their home port of Genoa in Italy. They made it only as far as Messina, on the island of Sicily, before the rapid spread of the disease forced them to stop.

This account of what happened in southern Ukraine may or may not be true. But it is a fact that the bubonic plague — the Black Death — arrived in Sicily in October 1347, carried by the crew of a fleet from the east. All the sailors on the ships were dead or dying. In the words of a **contemporary** historian, they had "sickness clinging to their very bones."

Draw Conclusions
Use what you have learned about the bubonic plague to explain why people called it the "Black Death."

---

contemporary alive during the same time period

The harbormasters at the port of Messina ordered the sick sailors to remain on board, hoping in this way to prevent the disease from spreading to the town. They had no way of knowing that the actual carriers of the disease had already left the ships. Under cover of night, when no one could see them, they had scurried down the ropes that tied the ships to the dock and vanished into Messina.

The carriers were black rats and the fleas that lived in their hair. Driven by an unending search for food, the rats' ancestors had migrated slowly westward along the caravan routes. They had traveled in bolts of cloth and bales of hay, and the fleas had come with them.

Although it was only an eighth of an inch long, the rat flea was a tough, adaptable creature. It depended for **nourishment** on the blood of its host, which it obtained through a daggerlike snout that could pierce the rat's skin. And in its stomach the flea often carried thousands of the deadly bacteria that caused the bubonic plague.

The bacteria did no apparent harm to the flea, and a black rat could **tolerate** a moderate amount of them, too, without showing ill effects.

---

nourishment food that a living thing needs to stay alive
tolerate put up with

What Do You Know?
Did you know that fleas could carry disease? What other insects do you know of that help spread disease?

English Coach
Host can mean "a person or a group that entertains guests." Here, *host* means "an animal on which another, smaller animal lives." Can you name some common animals that may be hosts for fleas?

But sometimes the flea contained so many bacteria that they invaded the rat's lungs or nervous system when the flea injected its snout. Then the rat died a swift and horrible death, and the flea had to find a new host.

Aiding the tiny flea in its search were its powerful legs, which could jump more than 150 times the creature's length. In most instances the flea landed on another black rat. Not always, though. If most of the rats in the **vicinity** were already dead or dying from the plague, the flea might leap to a human being instead. As soon as it had settled on the human's skin, the flea would begin to feed, and the whole process of infection would be repeated.

No doubt it was fleas, not Italian traders, that brought the bubonic plague to the Black Sea region, and other fleas that carried the disease on to Sicily. But no one at the time made the connection. To the people of the fourteenth century, the cause of the Black Death — which they called "the **pestilence**" — was a complete and utter mystery.

---

vicinity the area around a certain place
pestilence a deadly disease

Doctors at the time of the bubonic plague often wore "beaks" stuffed with spices or herbs, hoping to purify the air they breathed.

When the first cases of the plague were reported in Messina, the authorities ordered the Italian fleet and all its sick crew members to leave the port at once. Their action came too late, however. Within days the disease had spread throughout the city and the surrounding countryside.

Some of the plague's victims fled to the nearby town of Catania, where they were treated kindly at first. But when the citizens of Catania realized how deadly the disease was, they refused to have anything more to do with anyone from Messina or even to speak to them. As was to happen wherever the plague struck, fear for one's own life usually outweighed any concern a person might have felt for the life of another.

Think About It

You can check your understanding of the selection by asking yourself questions that begin with *Who? What? Where? When? Why?* and *How?* Reread as needed to find the answers to your questions.

How Does Nature Touch Lives?

How did nature touch lives during the time of the Black Plague? How did nature touch the lives of people who didn't get the disease? Does nature help spread diseases today? How does nature also help fight disease?

How Do I Measure Success?

A baby takes a first step. A child learns to ride a bike. A teen gets his or her first job. Each of these events is a success. Each person has accomplished a goal.

The characters and people you will read about in this unit experience success in different ways. Some of them weren't even looking for success, while others had to work hard to achieve it. As you read their stories, think to yourself, how are these people successful? How do I measure my own success?

La Causa

by Jessie Lopez de la Cruz

Have you ever fought for something that you believed in? What did you do to help your cause succeed? Jessie Lopez de la Cruz strongly believed in her cause — the fair treatment of farm workers. Jessie and her fellow workers faced dangerous situations as they fought for their rights, but they never gave up.

What Do You Know?
Have you ever seen or heard of workers who went on strike? Why did they strike? What did they do or say? Read on to see what the workers of La Causa did when they went on strike.

What Is La Causa?
La Causa, which means "The Cause," was started by a small group of **migrant** farm workers under the leadership of Cesar Chavez. In September 1965, Chavez led California grape pickers on a month-long strike that brought attention to the farm workers' fight for fair wages and better living conditions.

***

migrant a person who moves from one place to another

To fight against La Causa's strike, grape growers hired **"scab"** workers to pick the grapes. La Causa then took their protest into the community. They walked in front of supermarkets with picket signs, asking shoppers not to buy grapes. They also tried to make the scab workers leave the fields. These actions were meant to hurt the grape growers' ability to make a profit from their grapes.

Cesar Chavez speaking at a demonstration

The farm workers' **slogan** — "Viva la huelga!" ("Long live the strike!") — became known throughout the nation. La Causa grew to become the National Farm Workers Association, which later became the powerful United Farm Workers.

Jessie Lopez de la Cruz tells how she became involved in La Causa.

scab a worker who takes the job of a worker who is on strike

slogan a phrase that expresses the goals of a group

What's the Main Idea?
The main idea of this paragraph is stated clearly. Which sentence tells what the paragraph is mostly about?

It was very hard being a woman **organizer.** Many of our people my age and older were raised with the old customs in Mexico: where the husband rules, he is king of his house. The wife obeys, and the children, too. So when we first started it was very, very hard. Men gave us the most trouble — neighbors there in Parlier! They were for the union, but they were not taking orders from women, they said. . . .

We'd have a union meeting every week. Men, women, and children would come. Women would ask questions and the men would just stand back. I guess they'd say to themselves, "I'll wait for someone to say something before I do." The women were more **aggressive** than the men. And I'd get up and say, "Let's go on, let's do it! . . ."

The women took the lead for **picketing,** and we would talk to the people. It got to the point that we would have to find them, because the men just wouldn't go and they wouldn't take their wives.

Jessie Lopez (center) at a demonstration

organizer a person who gets workers to form a group or join a labor union
aggressive quick to take action
picketing standing together as a group to protest something

So we would say, "We're having our picket line at the Safeway in Fresno, and those that don't show up are going to have to pay a five-dollar fine." We couldn't have four or five come to a picket line and have the rest stay home and watch TV. In the end, we had everybody out there.

One time we were picketing — I think it was the early part of 1972 — White River Farms in Delano for a new contract. To go picket, we had to get up early. See, a lot of these growers were **chartering** buses, and at four or five o'clock in the morning they'd pick up the scabs. So we would follow these **labor bosses** who chartered the buses.

chartering renting or hiring
labor bosses people in charge of groups of workers

Draw Conclusions
Why would it be important for all workers to show up on the picket line during a strike?

English Coach
A contract is a formal agreement between people or groups. What may the growers and the migrant workers agree to in a contract?

At White River Farms one morning very early, we were out there by the hundreds by the road, and these people got down and started working out there in the grapes. We were asking them not to work, telling them that there was a strike going on. The grower had two guards at the entrance, and there was a helicopter above us. At other White River Farm ranches they had the sheriff, the county police, everybody. But there were pickets at three different ranches, and where we were picketing there wasn't anybody except these two guards. So I said, "Hey! What about the women getting together and let's rush 'em!" And they said, "Do you think we could do that?" And I said, "Of course we can! Let's go in there. Let's get 'em out of there any way we can." So about fifty of us rushed. We went under the vines. We had our banners, and you could see them bobbing up and down, up and down, and we'd go under those rows on our knees and roll over.

When the scabs saw us coming they took off. All of them went and they got on the bus. The guards had guns that they would shoot, and something black like smoke or **tear gas** would come out. That scared us, but we still kept on. After we saw all those workers get back on the buses, we went back.

Predict
Jessie suggests that the workers rush the field to chase off the scabs. What do you think will happen next? Will the workers succeed? What will the guards do?

tear gas a chemical gas that stings the eyes

Migrant worker
picking grapes

Instead of running this time, we rolled over and over all the way out. The vines are about four feet tall, and they have wire where you string up the vines. So you can't walk or run across one of these fences. You have to keep going under these wires. So I tripped, and rolled down about three or four rows before I got up. I rolled so they wouldn't get at me when they were shooting. When I got out there on the road they were getting these big, hard, dirty **clods** and throwing them at us. And then the **pickets** started doing the same thing. When the first police car came, somebody broke the windshield. We don't know if it was the scabs or someone on the picket lines, but the picketers were blamed.

Visualize It
What sentence helps you picture why the women have to go on their hands and knees or roll? Picture the actions of the women as they move through the field and describe what you see in your own words.

---

clods lumps of earth or clay
pickets people who are picketing; picketers

199

Character
From the information in this paragraph, what can you say about Jessie's character?

When we women ran into the fields, we knew we'd be arrested if they caught us. But we went in and we told the scabs, "If you're not coming out we're gonna pull you out!" Later I told [my husband] Arnold, "See? See what women can do? We got all those men out there to come out!"

A vineyard

At another place, in Kern County, we were sprayed with **pesticides.** They would come out there with their sprayers and spray us on the picket lines. They have these big tanks that are pulled by a tractor with hoses attached, and they spray the trees with this. They are strong like a water hose, but wider. They get it started and spray the vines and the trees. When we were picketing, they came out there to spray the pickets. What could we do? We tried to get as far away as we could, and then we would come back. They had goons with these big police dogs on leashes. I think they were trying to scare us by letting them loose on us. . . .

---

pesticides chemicals used to kill insects that destroy crops

English Coach
Goon is a word that can mean "a stupid person." *Goon* can also mean "someone hired to frighten or harm people." Which meaning do you think is intended here?

How Do I Measure Success?

Jessie Lopez de la Cruz says that it was very hard being a woman organizer. Do you think she was successful at the job? Why or why not? If the guards had stopped Jessie and the workers, would that change your answer? How may a person be successful even when his or her plans fail?

Hollywood and the Pits

by Cherylene Lee

Cherylene Lee became a child actor at the age of three. She appeared in television shows and two major films, acted in plays, and performed in a Las Vegas show with her sister. As you read, think about the ways that Cherylene and her mother measure success.

Predict
After you read the first paragraph, make predictions about what may happen in the selection. Will Cherylene enjoy her career in show business? Do you think Cherylene is still in show business today?

I suppose a lot of my getting into show business in the first place was a matter of luck — being in the right place at the right time. My sister, seven years older than me, was a member of the Meglin Kiddie Dance Studio long before I started lessons. Once during the annual **recital** held at the Shrine Auditorium, she was spotted by a Hollywood agent who handled only **Oriental** performers.

---

recital a music or dance performance
Oriental from a far-eastern country; Asian

202

The agent sent my sister out for a role in the CBS *Playhouse 90* television show *The Family Nobody Wanted*. The producer said she was too tall for the part. But true to my mother's training of always having a positive reply, my sister said to the producer, "But I have a younger sister . . ." which started my show-biz career at the tender age of three.

My sister and I were lucky. We enjoyed singing and dancing, we were natural hams, and our parents never discouraged us. In fact they were our biggest fans. My mother **chauffeured** us to all our dance lessons — lessons we begged to take. She drove us to interviews, took us to studios, went on location with us, drilled us on our lines, made sure we kept up our schoolwork and didn't **sass** back the **tutors** hired by studios to teach us for three hours a day. She never complained about being a stage mother. She said that we made her proud.

chauffeured drove people in a car
sass talk back to; show a lack of respect
tutors people who teach students outside of school

Cherylene (center) and her sister appear on a TV show with singer Dinah Shore.

English Coach
A ham is a person who overacts or shows off to get attention. What do you think the author means when she says that she and her sister were *natural hams*?

My father must have felt pride too, because he paid for a **choreographer** to put together our sister act: "The World Famous Lee Sisters," fifteen minutes of song and dance, real **vaudeville** stuff. We joked about that a lot, "Yeah, the Lee Sisters — Ug-Lee and Home-Lee," but we definitely had a good time. So did our parents.

In Las Vegas our sister act was part of a show called "Oriental Holiday." The show was about a Hollywood producer going to the Far East, finding **undiscovered** talent, and bringing it back to the U.S. We did two shows a night in the main showroom, one at eight and one at twelve, and on weekends a third show at two in the morning. It ran the entire summer often to standing-room-only audiences — a thousand people a show.

Our sister act worked because of the age and height difference. My sister then was fourteen and nearly five foot two; I was seven and very small for my age — people thought we were cute.

---

choreographer a person who plans the movements of a dance
vaudeville a stage show with many different short acts
undiscovered not found before; new

English Coach
"Ug-Lee" and "Home-Lee" are plays on words. "Home-Lee" sounds like *homely,* which means "plain or unattractive in appearance." What word does "Ug-Lee" sound like? What does the word mean?

A Las Vegas street in the 1960s

We had song-and-dance routines to old tunes like "Ma, He's Making Eyes at Me," "Together," and "I'm Following You," and my father hired a writer to adapt the **lyrics** to "I Enjoy Being a Girl," which came out "We Enjoy Being Chinese." We also told corny jokes, but the Las Vegas audience seemed to enjoy it. Here we were, two kids, staying up late and jumping around, and getting paid besides. To me the applause sometimes sounded like static, sometimes like distant waves. It always amazed me when people applauded. The owner of the hotel liked us so much, he invited us back to perform in shows for three summers in a row. That was before I grew too tall and the sister act didn't seem so cute anymore.

Context Clues
What do you think *corny* jokes are? What context clues help you figure out the meaning?

---

lyrics the words to a song

Cherylene with actor, dancer, and singer Gene Kelly

Cause and Effect Text Structure
What causes Cherylene to feel that making movies and doing shows isn't anything special? Look for a signal word to help you find the cause. What is the signal word?

I never felt my mother pushed me to do something I didn't want to do. But I always knew if something I did pleased her. She was generous with her praise, and I was sensitive when she withheld it. I didn't like to disappoint her.

I took to performing easily, and since I had started out so young, making movies or doing shows didn't feel like anything special. It was a part of my childhood — like going to the dentist one morning or going to school the next. I didn't wonder if I wanted a particular role or wanted to be in a show or how I would feel if I didn't get in. Until I was fifteen, it never occurred to me that one day I wouldn't get parts or that I might not "have what it takes."

When I was younger, I got a lot of roles because I was so small for my age. When I was nine years old, I could pass for five or six. I was really short. I was always teased about it when I was in elementary school, but I didn't mind because my height got me movie jobs. I could read and memorize lines that actual five-year-olds couldn't. My mother told people she made me sleep in a drawer so I wouldn't grow any bigger.

But when I turned fifteen, it was as if my body, which hadn't grown for so many years, suddenly made up for lost time. I grew five inches in seven months. My mother was amazed. Even I couldn't get used to it. I kept knocking into things, my clothes didn't fit right, I felt awkward and clumsy when I moved. Dumb things that I had gotten away with, like paying children's prices at the movies instead of junior admission, I couldn't do anymore. I wasn't a shrimp or a small fry any longer. I was suddenly normal.

Before that summer my mother had always claimed she wanted me to be normal. She didn't want me to become spoiled by the attention I received when I was working at the studios.

Make Inferences
What challenges may directors face when they try to find an actor to play a young child? Hint: Why did directors choose to hire Cherylene instead of hiring actual five-year-olds?

English Coach
A shrimp is a small sea animal related to the lobster. A fry is a newly hatched fish. How are the words *shrimp* and *small fry* used here?

I still had chores to do at home, went to public school when I wasn't working, was punished severely when I behaved badly. She didn't want me to feel I was different just because I was in the movies.

Cherylene Lee

But when she was sitting silently in all those waiting rooms while I was being turned down for one job after another, I could almost feel her wanting to shout, "Use her. Use her. What is wrong with her? Doesn't she have it anymore?" I didn't know what I had had that I didn't seem to have anymore. My mother had told the reporter that I was like everyone else. But when my life was like everyone else's, why was she disappointed?

More Information
Cherylene Lee went on to earn degrees in geology and paleontology. Later, she became a play writer, fiction author, and poet.

How Do I Measure Success?

Cherylene Lee was a successful child actor. How did she measure that success? How did her mother measure it? Think of something that you have succeeded at. Why do you feel that you succeeded? Did other people measure your success the same way that you did?

Have you ever sold a product door to door? Maybe you took part in a school fundraiser to sell candy, wrapping paper, or magazines. If so, you know that door to door is a difficult way to make sales. In these two selections, the main characters face both disappointment and success as they sell items door to door.

Dreamhouse

by R. Zamora Linmark

English Coach

Covered can mean "put over the surface of." It can also mean "traveled over." Which meaning is used in *chocolate-covered almonds*? Which meaning is used in the first line of the second paragraph?

I saw Steve Johnson's house for the first time last week. Florante, Mai-Lan, and Loata were helping me sell Jewel chocolate-covered almonds, the kind that came in a box with a two-dollar coupon from Pizza Hut wrapped around it. I needed to sell sixty boxes so I could go to Camp Erdman and participate in the Junior Police Officer's annual get-together.

After we nearly covered the entire valley and got the same response of sorry-just-bought-one, I told them I'd try once more before calling it quits.

I walked to the nearest house and knocked. A fat lady wearing glasses so thick they made her eyes look twenty-times bigger than the actual size, answered the door. I pulled out a box of Jewel's and was about to ask her if she wanted to buy some when she interrupted, "Too late. Just bought a case the other day. Too late."

We did an about-face and started to head back to my house when Mai-Lan came up with the idea of going to the far end of the valley where people like Steve Johnson live. "I'm sure we can sell everything in less than a minute," she said. "Yeah," Florante said, "maybe you might even win an **AM-FM headset.**"

It took us almost an hour's walk to reach the road that became narrower and narrower as the houses got bigger and bigger. The first doors we knocked on were all owned by Filipinos like Nelson Ariola's and Alan Vicente's families. We sold over twenty boxes in less than thirty minutes.

AM-FM headset a small radio with headphones

Predict
What type of people do you predict that *people like Steve Johnson* are? What kind of home do you think Steve Johnson lives in? Why? Write down your ideas. Then read on to see if you are right.

Draw Conclusions
What conclusion can you draw about how the group's success changes as the houses become bigger?

We ran excitedly through the next couple blocks, where the houses began to look more like a dream than wooden structures. Like Judy-Ann Kunishige's tea house in the middle of a lighted lily pond. Or Mr. and Mrs. Bernard Chun's indoor swimming pool with a Jacuzzi. We sold only ten boxes and it took us more than an hour's wait for them to decide. Only the Chuns didn't hesitate, because we are always spending our allowance in their store.

Mai-Lan counted the number of boxes sold. "Fifty-seven," she said. "Three more to go," Florante subtracted. "And one house left," I added. "That's o.k. We still have a chance," Loata said, pointing across the field to the biggest house in the valley. It seemed so far from us that it didn't look like a part of the valley. Or the valley didn't belong to it.

With the **sweltering** heat on our backs, we trudged across the field littered by gravel, broken bottles, and thorny weeds. We stopped in front of the gate and read the wooden sign drilled through the iron bars. Stenciled in fancy letterings were "No **Trespassing**" next to "Visitors, Please Ring Buzzer."

Loata rang the buzzer and we waited while Mai-Lan and Florante pressed their faces against the bars that **barricaded** the house. "It's so beautiful and so quiet, like a museum," she said. **"Miniature** rolling hills and Hollywood cars," he said. "A fountain of Cupid in the center of a pool," she said. "A walkway that unfolds like a wedding gown," he said. "It's a dreamhouse," she said. Loata pushed the button once more and did not let go. "Like Iolani Palace with department store windows," he said.

"It looks like Dillingham Prison," Loata blurted, finally releasing his finger off the buzzer. "I don't think anyone's home," I said. "But his parents' cars are there," he argued. "There's gotta be someone home." "Maybe they don't want to buy any chocolate," I said.

Context Clues
What do you think the word *stenciled* means? Look for clues in the sentence where *stenciled* appears. What clues help you figure out the meaning?

Visualize It
What phrases help you picture the house and the grounds? Does your image of the house change as you read? Why?

sweltering very hot and sticky
trespassing going onto someone's property without permission
barricaded blocked off in order to keep people or things out
miniature much smaller than normal

I did an about-face and started to walk back home when Florante shouted, "Look, there's Steve and his mom and dad." I turned around and saw the three of them standing behind the giant window. Like breathing **mannequins** on display. Steve and his mother smiling blankly, and his father blowing out smoke from the cigarette clipped between his fingers. Loata pressed the buzzer and we waited, our faces pushing against the bars.

But not one of them budged. They stood there posing like a Sears family portrait. We continued watching them until Steve's mother walked out of the picture and all we saw were bodies disappearing behind closing drapes. We stood there for I don't know how long, staring at the dreamhouse that was as far away as the hour it took us to get there and see them pretend that we were never there.

What's the Theme?
The narrator compares Steve's family to "breathing mannequins on display" and "a Sears family portrait." How do these comparisons support the theme of the selection? In your own words, what is the theme?

---

mannequins life-size models of people that are used to display clothes in stores

Door to Door

For more than 40 years, Bill Porter sold goods door to door for Watkins, a household products company. Porter chose to sell door to door despite the fact that he has **cerebral palsy.** But what makes Bill Porter truly exceptional are his **dedication** to his company, his devotion to his clients, and his belief in himself.

More Information
The Watkins company sells many home-care products, including laundry aids, all-purpose cleaners, personal-care products, pet-care items, and much more.

cerebral palsy a condition caused by damage to the brain that can affect movement and speech
dedication the state of being loyal and hardworking

A door-to-door salesman

215

English Coach
The base word in *unemployable* is *employ,* which means "to give a job to someone." The prefix *un-* means "not," and the suffix *-able* means "able to." What does *unemployable* mean?

When Bill Porter was growing up, people assumed that he was mentally disabled. At school he was placed in a class for slow learners. But although Porter had difficulty speaking, his brain functioned well. After he finished school, social service agencies told him that he was "unemployable." But his parents encouraged him to **persevere.** As Porter recalls, "The 'world' told me I could never earn an income, my mother told me I could, and my father told me I must!"

Porter applied for a sales job with Watkins, and when they said no, he wouldn't listen. Finally he was given a sales route that no one else wanted. At first the job was discouraging. Even in **inclement** weather, he walked about 10 miles per day, struggling with each step. Most people said no or simply closed the door on him, but Porter believed in his products. Eventually he became Watkins' top-selling salesperson.

---

persevere to continue trying to do something in a very determined way
inclement cold and wet

Bill Porter

Now Porter is over 70 years old, and he no longer sells door to door. But he is still as determined as ever, and he continues to sell goods for Watkins over the phone and the Internet. And he still won't take "no" for an answer.

Summarize It
Try to summarize what you have read about Bill Porter. First figure out what the selection was mostly about, then add only the most important details.

How Do I Measure Success?

How are the experiences of the characters in "Dreamhouse" and "Door to Door" similar? How are they different? Which character was most successful? Why do you think so? How would you measure your success if you sold items door to door?

Next Stop: Success
Teens learn to do business in the adult world

by Jocelyn Dong, the *Almanac*, 2001

Do you attend board meetings after school or develop cutting-edge advertising campaigns in the evenings? For teens involved in BUILD, a program that teaches them business and people skills, it's all part of success. These teens know how to turn dreams into reality.

Graphic Sources
Before you read, look ahead to find the headings that separate different parts of the selection. These headings can help you understand the structure of the text. They can also help you guess what you may read next.

Feeling like a basketball pro who'd just knocked off another game in the playoffs, Theron Jones reached across the polished oval table at Asset Management Company in Palo Alto, California, and shook hands with Bennett S. Dubin, **venture capital** partner, and his associate, Celim Yildizhan.

"Gentlemen, thanks," Mr. Jones said.

The meeting had gone well — exceptionally well.

---

venture capital the money needed to start a business

There in the conference room, Mr. Dubin had signed off on a second round of start-up funding for Mr. Jones's apparel company, SAV Clothing. The capital, desperately needed, would assure the company a smooth ride into the next year.

Talk had turned dicey at times, with Mr. Dubin raising the possibility of granting only part of the requested amount. But in the end, Mr. Jones made the slam dunk. He got the $1,325 he had come for.

Not bad for a 16-year-old **entrepreneur.**

Mr. Jones, also known as TJ, is part of BUILD of Menlo Park, California, an after-school nonprofit program that teaches teens the business skills needed to become entrepreneurs.

Context Clues
What is the meaning of the word *apparel?* What context clue helps you figure out this meaning?

---

entrepreneur a person who starts his or her own business

English Coach

An *indication* is "something that is a sign of something else." How do youths like TJ serve as an indication that BUILD is successful in preparing teens for work and giving them valuable life lessons?

If youths like TJ are any indication, BUILD is not only preparing teens for the working world, it's also giving them valuable life lessons about what it means to be an adult.

BUILD's CEO and president, Suzanne McKechnie Klahr, founded the **nonprofit** organization in 1999. Ms. McKechnie Klahr is a lawyer by training. But after working in public service, she quickly saw that low-income entrepreneurs needed help with business **fundamentals.**

At the same time, four high school students approached her for advice on starting a business. That's when BUILD (Businesses United in Investing, Lending, and Development) was born.

---

nonprofit not for the purpose of making money
fundamentals basic ideas

Business bootcamp

The program is not for the faint of heart. Students meet two to three times a week from September to May to learn business concepts and skills.

The two-year program is divided into two main classes, "E1" and "E2." The first year's curriculum, E1, introduces kids to business basics. The class finishes with a business-plan competition that brings in business **mentors** as judges. The prize money: $1,500 to start a business.

E2 takes over where E1 leaves off, moving the teens out of the classroom and into real-world situations where their skills are tested. TJ and eight other students are currently part of E2. They've been meeting with mentors, venture capitalists, and potential customers as they **implement** their business plans.

It sounds like a lot of work, and it is. And Ms. McKechnie Klahr would have it no other way.

---

mentors people who give advice; role models
implement put into action

English Coach
Look at the heading. *Bootcamp* refers to an intense training program for new soldiers. What do you think *business bootcamp* is? What might it be like?

"We made it clear we had extremely high expectations and clear boundaries. Students want high expectations. They will rise to the occasion. It's important not to sell these kids short," Ms. McKechnie Klahr said.

Those expectations include no more than three unexcused absences, no tardiness, homework, and occasional work on weekends. TJ puts in about 15 hours a week on his business, which sells hooded sweatshirts with his SAV brand.

Helping kids develop a professional manner is a key **aspect** of the program. Those who've worked with the teens have been impressed.

BUILD mentor Paul Javier recalled his first meeting with Amber Sade Bundy, who runs an image-consulting business and won the business-plan competition in May. When they met in September, Amber promptly gave him her business card.

Narrative or Informational?
Is the writing style of this selection narrative or informational? What clues help you decide? Hint: Narrative writing tells a story. Informational writing gives facts.

aspect part

"She handled herself like a mature adult professional," Mr. Javier said. "That's an excellent thing BUILD does for these kids."

The challenges of people

Perhaps one of the greatest challenges in the business world is learning how to deal with other people. For BUILD entrepreneurs, it has been no different.

Amber, who with a partner advises clothing stores on hot fashions for teens, called working with adults "very challenging."

"They're authority, and I have to hear what they're telling me," she said. "But it's hard to tell them that that's not what I'm looking for." She doesn't want to hurt anyone's feelings, she added.

Compare and Contrast
How are TJ and Amber alike? How are they different?

TJ acknowledged that teenagers get **intimidated** by adults. "When you look at adults, they're always rushing," TJ said. But hanging out with the folks at BUILD has **demystified** adults for TJ, and he's learned that, along with getting things done, adults want to have fun, too.

"They're big kids, with **priorities,**" he said.

TJ admits to wondering sometimes if he's letting his advisers push him around with their various suggestions. But he believes he's been able to strike a fair balance. "I don't let them push me. I accept their ideas. That's part of what being a CEO is," TJ said. "You gather ideas, analyze them, sort out the best stuff, and add creativity to give it that edge."

"Like no other experience"

For all the hours the teens put into the program, they say it's worth it. Amber got into the program because she wanted to have her own business and wouldn't have to rely on anyone else. She said she wanted "to have something with my name on it."

Make Inferences
What can you infer about the process that TJ uses to make decisions about his business?

---

intimidated worried and lacking confidence because of the situation or the people involved

demystified made a subject that seems difficult easier to understand

priorities tasks that are given the most importance

BUILD has given her that, along with helping her improve her people skills and organizational habits.

"It's like no other experience," she said.

Before BUILD, TJ had no interest in business whatsoever.

"When I saw what it was all about, it influenced me. I thought, 'I can do it.' And Suzanne said, 'Yeah, you can do it.' That's when I realized I was a natural entrepreneur," TJ said.

Now, more than a year into the program, TJ has learned to better manage his time. (In addition to BUILD, he works a part-time job and has his hands in DJ-ing and hairstyling.) And he's starting to sound like an experienced businessman.

English Coach
The expression *has his hands in* means "is involved in." What are some things that you have your hands in?

"When you go into a place, you gotta go in like, 'I own this place.' That's the type of attitude you have to have," he said.

Meanwhile, both Amber and TJ plan to continue growing their businesses.

"It's only logical for me to keep going on this venture," Amber said. She feels the pressure of a society that is looking for her, a young African-American woman, to fail. "It's up to me to prove them wrong."

TJ sees himself continuing the SAV Clothing line through his college years if possible. He knows there's a lot of work to be done before then.

Think About It
To check your understanding of what you have read, ask yourself questions that begin with *Who? What? Where? When? Why?* and *How?* Reread as needed to find the answers to questions you cannot answer easily.

How Do I Measure Success?

How did BUILD help TJ and Amber succeed? How did TJ and Amber measure their success? Would you like to take part in a program like BUILD? How might it help you succeed now? In the future? What type of business would you start? Why?

What Makes a Great Story?

What would you call a great story? What makes you keep turning the pages? Are you most interested in fast action? Spine-tingling suspense? Interesting characters? Intriguing mystery?

Not all great stories come from the imagination; sometimes they come from events that really happened. The selections you will read in this unit are all true, and they all have the elements of a great story. What makes a story great is not how real it is, but how well it is told.

The Story of a Shipwrecked Sailor

by Gabriel García Márquez

In 1955, a sailor, Luis Alejandro Velasco, was washed off the deck of his ship, along with seven of his crewmates. He spent the next ten days and nights drifting alone on a cork raft without food or fresh water. By Day 7 he was certain that his survival was up to him alone.

I don't know whether, after seven days without food and adrift at sea, one becomes accustomed to living that way. I think so. The hopelessness of the previous day was replaced by a mellow **resignation devoid** of emotion. I was sure that everything was different, that the sea and the sky were no longer hostile, and that the fish accompanying me on my journey were my friends. My old acquaintances of seven days.

---

resignation calm understanding that a situation cannot be changed

devoid completely without

228

    That morning I wasn't thinking about reaching any destination. I was certain that the raft had arrived in a region where there were no ships, where even sea gulls could go **astray.**

    I thought, however, that after seven days adrift I would become accustomed to the sea, to my anxious way of life, without having to spur my imagination in order to survive. After all, I had endured a week of harsh winds and waves. Why wouldn't it be possible to live on the raft **indefinitely?** The fish swam near the surface; the sea was clear and calm.

---

astray away from the right path
indefinitely for an unknown period of time

There were so many lovely, tempting fish around the raft it looked as if I could grab them with my hands. Not a shark was in sight. Confidently I put my hand in the water and tried to seize a round fish, a bright blue one about twenty centimeters long. It was as if I had flung a stone: all the fish fled instantly, momentarily churning up the water. Then slowly they came back to the surface.

You have to be crafty to fish with your hand, I thought. Underwater, the hand didn't have as much strength or **agility.** I chose one fish from the bunch. I tried to grab it. And in fact I did. But I felt it slip through my fingers with **disconcerting** speed and nimbleness. I waited patiently, not pressuring myself, just trying to catch a fish. I wasn't thinking about the shark which might be out there, waiting until I put my arm in up to the elbow so he could make off with it in one sure bite. I kept busy trying to catch fish until a little after ten o'clock. But it was useless. They nibbled at my fingers, gently at first, as when they nibble at bait. Then a little harder. A smooth silver fish about a foot and a half long, with **minute,** sharp teeth, tore the skin off my thumb. Then I realized that the nibbles of the other fish hadn't been harmless: all my fingers had small bleeding cuts.

agility ability to move quickly and easily
disconcerting upsetting and unexpected
minute tiny; pronounced as *my NOOT*

Shark in the raft!

I don't know if it was the blood from my fingers, but in an instant there was a riot of sharks around the raft. I had never seen so many. I had never seen them so **voracious.** They leaped like dolphins, chasing the fish and devouring them. Terrified, I sat in the middle of the raft and watched the **massacre.**

The next thing happened so quickly that I didn't realize just when it was that the shark leaped out of the water, thrashing its tail violently, and the raft, **tottering,** sank beneath the gleaming foam. In the midst of the huge, glittering wave that crashed over the side there was a metallic flash. **Instinctively** I grabbed an oar and prepared to strike a deathblow. But then I saw the enormous fin, and I realized what had happened. Chased by the shark, a brilliant green fish, almost half a meter long, had leaped into the raft. With all my strength I walloped it on the head with my oar.

---

voracious greedy; eating with a great appetite
massacre a brutal killing of many people or animals
tottering tipping back and forth
instinctively without thinking first

Killing a fish inside a raft isn't easy. The vessel tottered with each blow; it might have turned over. It was a **perilous** moment. I needed all my strength and all my wits about me. If I struck out blindly, the raft would turn over and I would plunge into a sea full of hungry sharks. If I didn't aim carefully, my **quarry** would escape. I stood between life and death. I would either end up in the gullet of a shark or get four pounds of fresh fish to appease the hunger of seven days.

I braced myself on the **gunwale** and struck the second blow. I felt the wooden oar drive into the fish's skull. The raft bounced. The sharks shuddered below. I pressed myself firmly against the side.

---

perilous extremely dangerous
quarry prey; a hunted animal
gunwale the upper edge of the side of a boat

When the raft **stabilized,** the fish was still alive. In agony, a fish can jump higher and farther than it otherwise can. I knew the third blow had to be a sure one or I would lose my prey forever.

After a lunge at the fish, I found myself sitting on the floor, where I thought I had a better chance of grabbing it. If necessary, I would have captured it with my feet, between my knees, or in my teeth. I anchored myself to the floor. Trying not to make a mistake and convinced that my life depended on my next blow, I swung the oar with all my strength. The fish stopped moving and a thread of dark blood tinted the water inside the raft.

I could smell the blood, and the sharks sensed it, too. Suddenly, with four pounds of fish within my grasp, I felt **uncontrollable** terror: driven wild by

the scent of blood, the sharks hurled themselves with all their strength against the bottom of the raft. The raft shook. I realized that it could turn over in an instant. I could be torn to pieces by the three rows of steel teeth in the jaws of each shark.

stabilized became steady
uncontrollable not able to be controlled or restrained

But the pressure of hunger was greater than anything else. I squeezed the fish between my legs and, staggering, began the difficult job of balancing the raft each time it suffered another assault by the sharks. That went on for several minutes. Whenever the raft stabilized, I threw the bloody water overboard. Little by little the water cleared and the beasts calmed down. But I had to be careful: a **terrifyingly** huge shark fin — the biggest I had ever seen — **protruded** more than a meter above the water's surface. The shark was swimming peacefully, but I knew that if it caught the scent of blood it would give a shudder that could **capsize** the raft. With extreme caution I began to try to pull my fish apart.

---

terrifyingly in a way that causes extreme fear
protruded stuck out
capsize tip over

What Makes a Great Story?

How did the author help to make this true tale a great story? How did Velasco feel after being at sea for seven days with no food or water? What happened to change that feeling? What kind of person does it take to survive such an ordeal? What would you do to survive under such conditions?

This Generation of Americans

by Frederick L. McKissack Jr.

The young people who lived through the Civil Rights Movement of the 1960s witnessed a tremendous shift in American society. This selection from a novel takes you back to that time. When thirteen-year-old Clay hears Dr. Martin Luther King Jr. give his historic "I Have a Dream" speech, he is changed forever.

The march is planned to begin about 11:30 at the Washington Monument at the east end of the Mall. It will proceed westward on either side of the reflecting pool about three quarters of a mile to the Lincoln Memorial where a number of speeches will be delivered. Most of us know that Martin Luther King's speech promises to be the highlight of the day.

We grab our signs and make our way to the Washington Monument at seven o'clock.

Thousands of marchers surround the Washington Monument and the reflecting pool on the National Mall.

Jake has changed from his traveling clothes into his "marching threads," a very snazzy double-breasted suit and a purple silk tie. I've changed into a clean shirt, but it's pretty rumpled from being in the bag all night.

Already there are a few hundred people at the monument, and we make our way over there to await the beginnings of the festivities. Jake and I stroll around to drink in the sights before it gets too crowded to move.

"Check out the goon squad," Jake says, jerking his chin in the direction of a grassy area near the Washington Monument. About 50 scrawny, scowling white guys, with their arms folded, stand there, just staring. They're surrounded by almost as many police officers.

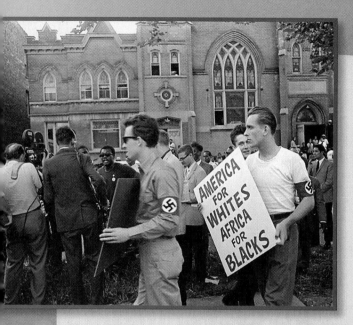

"Who are they?"

"**Nazis,**" says Jake. "I read in the paper they were planning to show up."

"What are they doing here?"

"Registering their disagreement, I guess," Jake says dryly.

Suddenly there's a **ruckus** from the direction of the buses. A rowdy group of teenagers, led by a tall guy in a bright red shirt, approaches us.

The tall guy claps and sings, "Freedom, freedom, freedom, freedom. Goin' to take it to the President."

And his followers sing, "Yeah, man."

The tall guy sings, "Goin' to take it to the Capital."

And his followers sing, "Yeah, man."

"Goin' to take it to the press."

"Yeah, man."

"Goin' to see it on the news."

Nazis individuals who believe that their race is superior to all others
ruckus a noisy uproar

"Yeah, man."

"Goin' to shout it from the mountain top."

"Shout it!"

This is better than I could have imagined. As the morning progresses, more and more people gather. There are people there from all over the country, and the world. We're in a sea of beautiful faces of every shade, most of them brown, but about every tenth one is white. There are old people, young people, nuns and priests, Muslims in head scarves, people in wheelchairs, some on crutches, pregnant women and babes in arms. All together, they are talking, singing, praying, laughing, shaking their signs. Some are rowdy and some are **serene.** Some are in their Sunday best. Others wear the uniforms of their work, or casual blue jeans. Some carry **parasols** for shade, while others tip their faces toward the sky like sunflowers.

serene peaceful
parasols small umbrellas that people carry for protection from sunlight

Demonstrators sit by the reflecting pool after the march on Washington.

But everyone, every single person there, walks with **dignity** and pride. In my mind, I compare these people — my people — to the Nazis, all ragged and **surly** and full of hate and out of place on their patch of grass, and it really hits me, all that we have to be proud of.

Then, at 11:20, the crowd starts to move. Without warning, and without instruction, it just decides, like it's one big organism, that it's time to march. We walk along, and it's mostly quiet. I can hear the shuffling of thousands of feet, and although we are shoulder to shoulder and the sun beats down on our heads, I feel cool and light, and suddenly I look over at Delia and I understand what Lo-Tone, Jake, and even John-Two, without knowing it, have been trying to explain to me; that the Tillborns were taking a stand in their own way, by knowing they belonged and never letting somebody else's **bigotry** shake that belief. And they were so firm in their belief that it didn't even put a dent in their joy, not for one second.

I work my way over to where Lo-Tone and Delia are walking. "Delia," I begin.

---

dignity self-respecting manner
surly rude and bad-tempered
bigotry hatred of a group of people because of their race, ethnicity, religion, or political views

She looks at me with no expression at all.

"Delia, I've been thinking. I know now I was wrong. And I know why I was wrong. And I hope you'll forgive me and be my friend."

She lowers her eyes, then raises them to mine. "There will be time for that, Clay. Now it's time to march." That's going to have to be good enough, for now.

The speeches all run together in my mind. I remember John Lewis, the founder of **SNCC,** and the fire and anger in his words of peace. I remember the singing of "We Shall Overcome." But most of all, as usual, I'm thinking about myself, and hoping it's not too late to make changes.

SNCC Student Nonviolent Coordinating Committee

Finally, it's announced that the next speaker is Dr. Martin Luther King Jr., who has just been released from a Montgomery jail for peaceful demonstrations.

Dr. King takes the **podium** and begins to speak: You can hear a pin drop on cotton. The wind snaps the American flag, and a jet hums overhead. But other than that, there are no other sounds, except the **affirmations** of the crowd as they respond to the emotions that Dr. King so elegantly expresses.

And the roar that arises from the crowd at the end of Dr. King's speech is like nothing I've ever heard, or, I will come to learn, like anything I will ever hear again. It's a roar of joy, of longing, of pride and sadness, a roar that wraps itself around every wound, every scar, every fear in the heart of every man, woman, and child in that crowd, and flings it upward, to heaven, in one full-throated, **beseeching** bellow of hope.

podium a platform or stand that a person speaks from

affirmations statements of approval and agreement

beseeching asking in a very serious way

Martin Luther King Jr. delivering his famous "I Have a Dream" speech

And then, remarkably, it's over. There's nothing much to say to add to what we've just shared, and we make the short walk back to the buses in silence and pile on. We are, to say the least, exhausted. But filled with something that we all know will never go away, I stow my bag above my seat and slide in next to the window. I saw Jake in line for the comfort station, so I figure he's changing back into his traveling clothes. I look out the window at the thinning crowd.

"Is this seat taken?"

I know before I look up that it's Delia.

"No . . . no, it's not," I say. "It's . . . it's . . ."

"Free?" she smiles.

Yes, that's the word.

What Makes a Great Story?

How can you tell that the narrator of this selection believed that his experience in Washington, D.C., made a great story? Do you agree that it's a great story? If you could witness an event in the past or in the future that you think would be a great story, what event would you choose? Why?

On September 11, 2001, terrorists attacked New York City, Washington, D.C., and Shanksville, Pennsylvania. People everywhere struggled to make sense of the tragic events. All were saddened by the news; most were confused by their feelings. Sam Hester, a cartoonist, shows all of the emotions she felt after learning about the attacks.

FIRST REACTION: A KNOT OF HORRIBLE FEAR IN MY STOMACH — BEFORE A DOZEN SECOND-REACTIONS EXPLODED IN MY MIND

nocturnal active at night

pad thai a stir-fried noodle dish from Thailand
layovers short stops between flights

emotionally with strong feelings

dispassionately calmly; without strong feelings

trivial of little value or importance
acute sharp; severe

dystopic related to an imaginary place where life is extremely difficult

morbid grim or ghastly

What Makes a Great Story?

How did Sam Hester react to the events of September 11, 2001? How were her feelings similar to and different from your own? How did her feelings change over time? Do you agree that "time heals pain"? Why or why not?

Rocket Man

The Space Age officially began in 1957, but space remained off-limits to all but the most highly trained astronauts. In 2004, the non-government craft SpaceShipOne made history by sending pilot Mike Melvill into space. But SpaceShipOne had problems as soon as the rockets fired. What was the fate of this first flight?

On June 21, 2004, at around 3 a.m., a crowd begins to gather near the Mojave Airport in California's Mojave Desert. A few hours later, about 27,000 people have arrived. Winds are brisk, but as dawn approaches everyone can see that the skies are beautiful and clear. The massive crowd is **abuzz** with excitement: They hope that today they will witness history in the making.

The crowd awaits the launch of SpaceShipOne. If the flight succeeds, it will be the first privately funded flight to leave Earth's **atmosphere.**

---

abuzz filled with talk and activity
atmosphere the air surrounding Earth

Paul Allen, Mike Melvill, and Burt Rutan in front of SpaceShipOne

Government programs, such as the National Aeronautics and Space Administration (NASA) in the United States, have funded all previous space flights. The research, design, construction, and testing of SpaceShipOne have all been funded by Paul Allen, who co-founded Microsoft Corporation and is now an **investor** and **philanthropist. Aviation** designer Burt Rutan designed the ship, and record-holding pilot Mike Melvill will be at the controls during the flight.

---

investor a person who puts money into a business to make a profit
philanthropist a person who gives time and money to helping others
aviation the science that builds and flies aircraft

SpaceShipOne has already achieved one aviation **milestone:** On May 13, just over one month earlier, it climbed to 211,400 feet (about 40 miles), the highest **altitude** ever reached by a non-government space flight program. Everyone present today hopes that the ship will shatter its own record by climbing to an altitude of 62 miles, beyond Earth's atmosphere.

At about 6 a.m., the steel doors of an **airport hangar** open to reveal a sleek, shining white spaceship. The ship consists of two separate parts — SpaceShipOne, the ship that will soon fly into space, and the White Knight, the "mothership."

---

milestone an important event or turning point
altitude the height above any given point
airport hangar a shelter used to store aircraft

The excited crowd waits for the launch of SpaceShipOne.

The larger White Knight will carry the smaller SpaceShipOne into the air, and then will release the smaller craft for its flight into space.

The launch is scheduled to take place at 6:30 a.m., but as that time approaches, it becomes clear that there will be a slight delay. However, the anxious crowd is assured that the flight is still expected to proceed. At 6:32 a.m., the engines of the mothership are started, and the craft begins to roll towards the runway. Hundreds of photographers and **journalists clamor** to capture the events as they take place. Some reporters send e-mail updates to their headquarters every few minutes. Hopeful vendors sell T-shirts **commemorating** the historic flight before it has even taken place.

At about 6:47 a.m., the White Knight finally roars into the sky, carrying SpaceShipOne along with it. The ships circle above the airport as they climb higher and higher into the sky. As they gain altitude, they appear to grow smaller to the cheering crowd below.

---

journalists people who work to get the news to the public
clamor to make loud and continuous noise
commemorating honoring or remembering a person or event

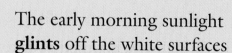

The early morning sunlight **glints** off the white surfaces of the spacecrafts, making them beacons to the crowd below. About 45 minutes after the launch, viewers begin to see a white **contrail** following the White Knight through the sky. Soon SpaceShipOne will be released.

Finally, at about 7:50 a.m., the ships reach an altitude of 47,000 feet, and the White Knight sets SpaceShipOne free. For a few seconds, SpaceShipOne glides in freefall mode, and the crowd members hold their breath. Then Mike Melvill fires the ship's rockets, and SpaceShipOne hurtles toward space at incredible speed. The relieved crowd cheers when they see the rocket firing. Fortunately, they cannot see what happens just after Melvill fires the rockets. High in the air, the unsteady spacecraft rolls 90 degrees to the left and then 90 degrees to the right. This takes Melvill by surprise, and he works to regain control of the ship as it flies upward.

---

glints gleams or flashes
contrail a trail of water droplets left by an aircraft as it flies through the air, usually visible from the ground

During the late rocket-burning phase, one of the ship motors **malfunctions,** leaving the ship unbalanced. Melvill quickly switches to a backup system, but the problems have already affected the ship. The ship is now climbing at a different angle, and new problems may lie ahead.

Around 8:00 a.m., about an hour and fifteen minutes after the launch, Mike Melvill and SpaceShipOne push through the atmosphere and into space. A mission official on the ground announces that everything looks good. However, the ship stops short of its target altitude of 360,000 feet, climbing to only 328,491 feet. Melvill hears a loud bang coming from the engine area of the ship, where a piece holding the nozzle of the craft has buckled. Despite these problems, the ship is in space: Melvill and the SpaceShipOne team have made history.

SpaceShipOne remains in space for only three minutes, but Melvill makes the most of his time there. As the crowd waits 62 miles below, Melvill reaches into a pocket of his flight suit and pulls out a handful of M&M candies. He releases them and watches them float weightlessly in the cockpit.

---

malfunctions fails to work properly

Mike Melvill in the cockpit of SpaceShipOne

He also takes a minute to gaze through the portholes at Earth below and space above. Melvill will later tell people, "Looking out that window, seeing the white clouds in the LA Basin, it looked like [there was] snow on the ground." But for now Melvill has no one to talk to — he is separated from his fellow human beings by 62 miles of empty space, **ozone,** and atmosphere.

As quickly as Melvill entered space, it is time to begin his descent. As SpaceShipOne glides back into the atmosphere, Melvill flips a switch that causes SpaceShipOne's large tail section to rise up. This slows the spacecraft down as it approaches the ground for its landing. In a victory lap, SpaceShipOne circles above the airport to the cheers of the crowd below.

---

ozone a form of oxygen in the air around Earth

At about 8:15 a.m., SpaceShipOne lands on the same runway it took off from less than two hours earlier. It has journeyed to space and back, and Mike Melvill has officially earned his **commercial** astronaut wings. Members of the crowd shout joyfully and punch the air in triumph.

As Melvill climbs out of the cockpit, he spots a familiar face: Buzz Aldrin, one of the two astronauts who walked on the moon during the Apollo XI space mission of 1969. Aldrin shakes Melvill's hand, congratulating him and welcoming him to a very **exclusive** club — the small group of human beings who have entered outer space.

---

commercial related to private business, not government
exclusive not shared with many others

What Makes a Great Story?

Do you think the first flight of SpaceShipOne makes a great story? Why or why not? What were the important events in the story of SpaceShipOne? Which events did you find the most exciting? How do you think the future of space exploration may change as a result of SpaceShipOne's flight? What makes a real-life event a great story?

Acknowledgments

Acknowledgment is gratefully made to the following publishers, authors, and agents for permission to reprint or adapt these works. Every effort has been made to determine copyright owners. In the case of any omissions, the Publisher will be pleased to make suitable acknowledgments in future editions.

Adapted from "Kids and Extreme Sports" by Kyanna Sutton. Permission granted by www.FamilyEducation.com © 2000–2005 Pearson Education, Inc. All Rights Reserved.

"Right Kick, Wrong Direction," reprinted by permission of Joseph Losardo. Copyright © 2001 Joseph Losardo.

"Black Hair" from *New and Selected Poems* by Gary Soto. Copyright © 1995 by Gary Soto. Used with permission of Chronicle Books LLC, San Francisco. Visit ChronicleBooks.com.

Excerpts from "Striving to make music under the streets of NYC" by Daniel Streiff and Jon Sweeney. MSNBC, August 26, 2004. © 2005 MSNBC Interactive. Reprinted by permission of Daniel Streiff.

"The Song of Stones River" from *What a Song Can Do* by Jennifer Armstrong, copyright © 2004 by Jennifer Armstrong. Used by permission of Alfred A. Knopf, an imprint of Random House Children's Books, a division of Random House, Inc.

Adapted from "Leaving 'El Combito'" by Angy Gonzalez. Copyright © 2005 by Youth Communication. Reprinted by permission.

From *Real Boys' Voices,* by William Pollack, copyright © 2000 by William Pollack. Used by permission of Random House, Inc.

"Sailing Away" from *Necessary Noise,* by Michael Cart. Copyright © 2003 by Michael Cart. Used by permission of HarperCollins Publishers.

From *Cat's Eye* by Margaret Atwood. Copyright © 1988 by O.W. Toad Ltd. Reprinted by permission of Random House, Inc.

Adapted from "Mix It Up: The Trouble with Fitting In" by Liia Rudolph, from *Mix It Up Stories,* copyright © 2005, Tolerance.org. Reprinted by permission of Teaching Tolerance.

From "Their Own Om: Yoga For Teens" by Bess Gallanis. Reprinted by permission of Yoga Chicago and Bess Gallanis.

"Getting a Kick Out of Martial Arts" by Mariana Relos. *Current Health,* January 2004. Copyright © January 2004, Weekly Reader Corporation. Reprinted by permission of WRC Media Inc.

From "The Crash Room" by David Rice. Copyright © 1997 by David Rice. Reprinted by permission of the author.

Excerpt from "An exchange student at 17" by Elaine Abonal. Reprinted by permission of InternationalStudent.com.

Text for Annemarie Brown's "Outward Bound" was provided by the Environmental Education Council of Marin's Teen Environmental Media Network, 1005 A Street, Suite 202, San Rafael, CA 94901. Learn more about their hands-on journalism program at temn@eecom. net or (415) 485-4908 or www.eecom.net.

From "The Flying Fool" by Thomas Fleming. Reprinted by permission of the author.

"Whirlwind Survivors" by James A. Fussell. *The Kansas City Star*, May 4, 2002. Copyright © 2002 Knight Ridder. Reprinted by permission.

Susan Power, excerpt from "Chicago Waters" in *Roofwalker* (Minneapolis: Milkweed Editions, 2002). Copyright © 2002 by Susan Power. Reprinted with permission from Milkweed Editions.

"Booming Ground" by Ray Gonzalez. Reprinted by permission of the author.

"The Rain Came" by Grace Ogot. Reproduced with permission from East African Educational Publishers Ltd.

From *When Plague Strikes: The Black Death, Smallpox, AIDS* by James Cross Giblin. Copyright © 1995 by James Cross Giblin. Used by permission of HarperCollins Publishers.

"Hollywood and the Pits" by Cherylene Lee. Copyright © 1992 by Cherylene Lee. Reprinted by permission of Bret Adams Ltd.

"Dreamhouse" by R. Zamora Linmark. Reprinted by permission of the author.

From "Next Stop: Success. Teen entrepreneurs learn to do business in the adult world," by Jocelyn Dong. *The Almanac.* Copyright © 2001 Embarcadero Publishing Company. Reprinted by permission.

From *The Story of a Ship-Wrecked Sailor* by Gabriel García Márquez, translated by Randolph Hogan, copyright © 1986 by Alfred A. Knopf, Inc. Used by permission of Random House, Inc.

From *This Generation of Americans* by Frederick L. McKissack Jr. Copyright © 2000 by Frederick L. McKissack Jr. Jamestown Publishers, a division of NTC/Contemporary Publishing Group, Inc.

"September 11," reprinted by permission of Sam Hester.

Photo Credits

COVER (l)Stockbyte Platinum/Alamy Images, (r)Getty Images/
PunchStock, (bkgd)Getty Images; **1** CORBIS; **2** ORLANDO KISSNER/
AFP/Getty Images; **5** Eric Meola/Getty Images; **6** Jim Campbell/Areo
News Network/Pool/Reuters/CORBIS; **7** Getty Images; **9** StockShot/
Alamy Images; **11** CORBIS; **12** S. P. Gillette/CORBIS; **13** Galen
Rowell/CORBIS; **14** Grafton Marshall Smith/CORBIS; **16** Las Cruces
Sun-News, Vladimir Chaloupka/AP/Wide World Photos; **17** Jacques
Boissinot/AP/Wide World Photos; **18 19** Duomo/CORBIS; **20** Donald
Miralle/Getty Images; **23** Michael Kevin Daly/CORBIS; **24** Alamy
Images; **25** Chris Willson/Alamy Images; **26** Michael Newman/
PhotoEdit; **28** Jim Cummins/CORBIS; **31** Bettmann/CORBIS; **32**
Courtesy of Marie Pepe; **34** Jim McKnight/AP/Wide World Photos;
35 Marc Vaughn/Masterfile; **37** Getty Images; **39** Sarma Ozols/Getty
Images; **40** John Stanton/Getty Images; **42** Brand X; **44** Colin Hawkins/
Getty Images; **45** Peter Beavis/Getty Images; **47** Courtesy of Theo
Eastwind; **49** Kike Calvo/V&W/The Image Works; **50** Mary Altaffer/
AP/Wide World Photos; **52** ©2005 Mark Lee Blackshear; **55** Marian
Anderson Collection, Rare Book & Manuscript Library, University of
Pennsylvania; **56** Tomas D. McAvoy/Time & Life Pictures/Getty Images;
58 Bettmann/CORBIS; **60** Library of Congress; **63** Smithsonian
American Art Museum, Washington, DC/Art Resource, NY; **64**
CORBIS; **65 67** Library of Congress; **68** Raymond Gehman/CORBIS;
69 Rubberball; **70** Jeff Greenberg/PhotoEdit; **71** Alamy Images; **72**
Robert Frerck/Odyssey Productions; **73** ORLANDO KISSNER/AFP/
Getty Images; **74** CORBIS; **76** BananaStock/Alamy Images; **78** Michael
Newman/PhotoEdit; **79** David Woolley/Getty Images; **80** Janine Wiedel
Photolibrary/Alamy Images; **82** Getty Images; **85** Greg Gilman/Alamy
Images; **87** Alan Schein Photography/CORBIS; **89** Gail Mooney/
Masterfile; **90** CORBIS; **93** Medioimages/Getty Images; **95** Chris Rout/
Bubbles Photo Library; **96** Getty Images; **97** CORBIS; **98** Alamy Images;
99 Rubberball; **101** Bonnie Kamin/PhotoEdit; **103** David Young-Wolff/
PhotoEdit; **105** Megan Maloy/Getty Images; **106** Davis Barber/
PhotoEdit; **107** David Young-Wolff/PhotoEdit; **109** Ed Kashi/CORBIS;

110 Daniel Berehulak/Getty Images; 112 113 ©2006 Intuitive Surgical, Inc.; 114 NASA; 117 Gary Conner/PhotoEdit; 118 Keren Su/China Span; 120 Yun Jai-Hyoung/AP/Wide World Photos; 121 Tony Freeman/ PhotoEdit; 123 Brian Summers/First Light; 125 127 Alamy Images; 128 Getty Images; 129 Yoav Levy/PhotoTake NYC; 130 Sean Justice/Getty Images; 131 Rubberball; 133 Richard Hamilton Smith/CORBIS; 134 135 Courtesy Elaine Abonal; 137 Catherine Karnow/CORBIS; 138 Conde Nast Archive/CORBIS; 141 Alamy Images; 142 Michael DeYoung/CORBIS; 143 Ray Wheeler; 145 Brian Bailey/CORBIS; 147 Bettmann/CORBIS; 149 Underwood & Underwood/CORBIS; 150 Bettmann/CORBIS; 152 (l)Culver Pictures, Inc./SuperStock, (r)David J. & Janice L. Frent Collection/CORBIS; 155 North Wind Picture Archives; 156 Bettmann/CORBIS; 158 North Wind Picture Archives; 159 Bettmann/CORBIS; 161 Rubberball; 163 Eric Nguyen/Ji, Redd Photo/ CORBIS; 165 The Topeka Capital-Journal; 166 168 169 Kansas City Library; 171 Photri/Li Balterman; 173 Churchill & Klehr; 174 Rebecca Dallinger; 176 Hubert Stadler/CORBIS; 179 Charles & Josette Lenars/ CORBIS; 180 Zute Lightfoot/Alamy Images; 183 Wendy Stone/ CORBIS; 185 Eric Meola/Getty Images; 187 Fogg Art Museum, Harvard University Museums/Bridgeman Art Library; 189 MAPS.com/ CORBIS; 191 Getty Images; 192 SuperStock, Inc./SuperStock; 193 Rubberball; 195 Jason Laure/The Image Works; 196 ©1976 George Ballis/Take Stock; 197 Paul Fusco/Magnum Photos; 199 ©1976 Bob Fitch/Take Stock; 200 Sergio Pitamitz/zefa/CORBIS; 203 Courtesy of Cherylene Lee; 205 SuperStock; 206 208 Courtesy of Cherylene Lee; 211 Alamy Images; 212 Wes Thompson/CORBIS; 214 Steve Skjold/ Alamy Images; 215 Tim Bradley/Getty Images; 217 Angela Pancrazio/ The Oregonian; 219 Jeff Greenberg/PhotoEdit; 220 Peter Dazeley/ Getty Images; 222 Getty Images; 223 Jeff Greenberg/PhotoEdit; 225 Myrleen Ferguson Cate/PhotoEdit; 227 Rubberball; 229 The Mariner's Museum/CORBIS; 230 CORBIS; 231 Stephen Frink/zefa/CORBIS; 233 Stuart Westmorland/Getty Images; 234 Tobias Bernard/zefa/ CORBIS; 237 Flip Schulke/CORBIS; 238 AP/Wide World Photos; 239 Bettmann/CORBIS; 241 CORBIS; 242 Bob Adelman/Magnum Photos; 244-251 Sam Hester; 253 Mike Blake/Reuters/CORBIS; 254 Robyn Beck/AFP/Getty Images; 256 Jim Campbell/Areo News Network/Pool/ Reuters/CORBIS; 258 Discovery Channel/Vulcan Productions/AP/ Wide World Photos; (bkgd)Getty Images.